MULTITUDES

by JOHN HOLLINGWORTH

Multitudes was first performed at the Tricycle Theatre, London,
on 19 February 2015

TRICYCLE THEATRE
A local theatre with an international presence

The Tricycle views the world through a variety of lenses, bringing unheard voices into the mainstream. It presents high-quality and innovative work, which provokes debate and emotionally engages. Located in Brent, the most diverse borough in London, the Tricycle is a local venue with an international vision.

The Tricycle Theatre produces world-class British and international theatre that reflects the rich diversity of the local community.

We present theatre that crosses different continents, voices and styles, theatre that tells stories about how human connections are made through differences of culture, race or language.

Recent productions include *The House That Will Not Stand* by Marcus Gardley; the Olivier Award-winning *Handbagged* by Moira Buffini, which transferred to the West End; and the critically acclaimed *Red Velvet* by Lolita Chakrabarti (winner of two Critics' Circle Awards and an Evening Standard Award), which transferred to New York.

The Tricycle Theatre has also collaborated with companies including Sundance Theatre Lab, Tiata Fahodzi, Complicite, Liverpool Everyman and Eclipse Theatre.

Our ambitious Creative Learning programme aims to develop the imagination, aspiration and potential of children and young people. We invest in creating meaningful relationships with young people sometimes described as 'harder to reach' or who are passionate about theatre but have limited access to it.

/tricycletheatre

@TricycleTheatre

www.tricycle.co.uk

A WELCOME FROM THE DIRECTOR

I first worked with John Hollingworth when he was part of the *Women, Power and Politics* cast at the Tricycle in 2010. A year later he asked if I would direct a workshop of his first play at the National Theatre Studio. At this time the play had a different name but bore the seeds of what would become *Multitudes*.

I found it refreshing that, as a playwright, John wanted to write about the multicultural Britain that he grew up in, and which has informed him so much as an artist. When I became Artistic Director, I immediately commissioned him.

When I read the first draft of the script, I enjoyed how John transported us to a diverse Bradford, a city that he loves, as well as a world of religious conversions and political conferences. Here was a story I had not seen told in this way before.

The play has been on a huge journey, and I am proud to be presenting another world premiere by a first-time playwright.

This play was programmed to coincide with the run-up to the General Election, though recent global events are now throwing another light on the subject matter explored. *Multitudes* feels an even more pertinent and important story today, and will hopefully provoke dialogue and discussion.

We want the Tricycle to be a place where we share bold and vital stories that give a voice to many sides of a complex issue; bringing together all the communities that we serve here in Brent as a united audience.

I hope you enjoy today's performance and look forward to welcoming you back to the Tricycle again.

Indhu Rubasingham

Indhu Rubasingham
Artistic Director
Tricycle Theatre

MULTITUDES

by John Hollingworth

CAST

Natalie	Clare Calbraith
Kash	Navin Chowdhry
Qadira	Salma Hoque
Imtiaz/Amir/Julian/Shafiq	Asif Khan
Lyn	Jacqueline King
Rukhsana/Sam/Harpreet/Monica/Waitress/Sister	Maya Sondhi

CREATIVE TEAM

Director	Indhu Rubasingham
Designer	Richard Kent
Lighting Designer	Oliver Fenwick
Sound Designers	Ben & Max Ringham
Movement Director	Lucy Hind
Assistant Director	Harry Mackrill
Voice/Dialect Coach	Richard Ryder
Fight Director	Kevin McCurdy
Production Manager	Shaz McGee
Company Stage Manager	Helen Knott
Deputy Stage Manager	Emma Tooze
Assistant Stage Manager	Imogen Firth
Rehearsal Assistant Stage Manager	Michael Fraser
Costume Supervisor	Emily Barratt
Make-up Artist	Emma Procter
Chief Electrician	Paul Kizintas
Head of Sound	Mike Thacker
Lighting Board Operator	Ben Jones
Wardrobe Mistress	Jessica Bishop
Set Built by	R!diculous Solut!ons
Scenic Artist	Paul Wallis
Crew	Seb Cannings, Tom Frances, Liam Hill, Emma Hughes, Alfie O'Brien, Sam Stuart, Tim de Vos
Casting Director	Anna Cooper
Press Representation	Kate Morley PR

THE WRITER

John Hollingworth

John was born in Keighley and went to school in Bradford. He read English at Trinity College, Dublin and trained as an actor at RADA. This is his first full-length play.

Writing credits include: *Animal Wrongs* (Arcola); *Broken Window Theory* (Soho); *Blue Yonder* (Tristan Bates).

Acting credits include:

For the Tricycle: *Women, Power and Politics.*

Theatre includes: *An Intervention* (Paines Plough); *Our Country's Good* (Out of Joint); *Making Noise Quietly* (Donmar Warehouse); *Earthquakes in London* (National Theatre/Headlong); *The Deep Blue Sea* (West Yorkshire Playhouse); *Design for Living* (Old Vic); *The Power of Yes* (National Theatre); *Observe the Sons of Ulster Marching Towards the Somme* (Hampstead); *For King and Country* (Theatre Royal Plymouth/UK tour); *The Playboy of the Western World* (Nuffield, Southampton).

Television includes: *Josh, Arthur & George, Poldark, Our World War, Crossing Lines, Da Vinci's Demons, Breathless, Endeavour, The Hour, London's Burning, The Man Who Crossed Hitler, Twenty Twelve, Casualty 1909, Being Human, Wuthering Heights.*

Film includes: *Tarzan the Untamed, Cinderella, About Time, The Dark Knight Rises, The Burma Conspiracy, Godard & Others, Pelican Blood, Dorian Gray.*

CAST

Clare Calbraith
Natalie

Theatre includes: *Last Days of Troy* (Royal Exchange, Manchester/ Shakespeare's Globe); *Neighbors* (HighTide); *Saturday Night and Sunday Morning* (Royal Exchange, Manchester); *Hangover Square* (Finborough); *Humble Boy* (New Victoria); *A Doll's House* (Northcott, Exeter); *The Merchant of Venice, King Lear, The Mysteries* (Northern Broadsides); *The Cherry Orchard, Don Juan* (ETT).

Television includes: *Home Fires, Silent Witness, Vera, Downton Abbey, The Shadow Line, 55 Degrees North.*

Navin Chowdhry
Kash

Theatre includes: *The Night Before Christmas* (Soho); *Shades, Behind the Image* (Royal Court); *Much Ado About Nothing* (Shakespeare's Globe); *Night Sky* (Old Vic).

Television includes: *Babylon, A Touch of Cloth, The Job Lot, New Tricks, Reunited, Five Days, NY-Lon, Doctor Who, Teachers, Dalziel & Pascoe, Synchronicity.*

Film includes: *Happy New Year, Skellig, Red Mercury, The Seventh Coin, Madame Sousatzka.*

Salma Hoque
Qadira

Theatre includes: *Drawing the Line* (Hampstead); *Sick Rooms* (NYT).

Television includes: *FAM, Holby City.*

Asif Khan
Julian/Amir/ Shafiq/Imtiaz

Theatre includes: *Snookered* (Bush/ Tamasha); *Mixed Up North* (Out of Joint); *Kabaddi Kabaddi Kabaddi* (Arcola); *Queen of the Nile* (Hull Truck); *Twelfth Night* (National Theatre); *The Snow Queen, The Nutcracker & The Mouse King* (Unicorn).

Television includes: *Spooks, Going Postal, The Dumping Ground, Dark Matters, Casualty, Bradford Riots.*

Film includes: *Dumpee.*

Jacqueline King
Lyn

Theatre includes: *Life for Beginners* (Theatre503); *Beyond the Horizon /Spring Storm* (National Theatre/ Royal & Derngate, Northampton); *Larkin With Women, Major Barbara, Press Cuttings, The Madras House* (Orange Tree); *Damsel in Distress, Comic Potential* (West End); *10 x 10 season* (Stephen Joseph, Scarborough); *Wuthering Heights* (West Yorkshire Playhouse); *Much Ado About Nothing* (Oxford Playhouse).

Television includes: *Silk, Give Out Girls, George Gently, Doctor Who* (Series 4), *Missing, House of Saddam, 55 Degrees North* (Series 1 and 2), *Midsomer Murders.*

Film includes: *Writers' Retreat, The Prince of Hearts, Mayflower – Dangerous Crossing.*

Jacqueline has recorded over 250 unabridged books and has toured to Canada, Nairobi, UAE, Germany, Holland and Sri Lanka.

Maya Sondhi
Rukhsana/Sam/ Harpreet/Monica /Waitress/Sister /Surgeon

Theatre includes: *There* (Royal Court); *Yerma* (Arcola); *Bollywood Cinderella* (Tara Arts); *A Bold Stroke for a Husband* (Bridewell); *The Massacre* (Theatre Royal, Bury St. Edmunds).

Television includes: *Citizen Khan, Silent Witness, Judge John Deed, Collision, Doctors, Family Affairs, Casualty, Fair City.*

Writing includes: *The Kumars* (Sky1).

CREATIVES

Indhu Rubasingham
Director

Indhu is the Artistic Director of the Tricycle Theatre.

As Artistic Director: *The House That Will Not Stand; Handbagged* (Tricycle/West End, Olivier Award for Outstanding Achievement in an Affiliate Theatre); *Paper Dolls; Red Velvet* (Tricycle/St Ann's Warehouse New York, Evening Standard Award and Critics' Circle Award).

For the Tricycle: *Women, Power and Politics; Stones in His Pockets; Detaining Justice; The Great Game: Afghanistan; Fabulation; Starstruck.*

Other selected directing credits include: *Belong, Disconnect, Free Outgoing, Lift Off, Clubland, The Crutch, Sugar Mummies* (Royal Court); *Ruined* (Almeida); *Yellowman, Anna in the Tropics* (Hampstead);*The Waiting Room* (National Theatre); *The Ramayana* (National Theatre/Birmingham Rep); *Secret Rapture, The Misanthrope* (Minerva, Chichester); *Romeo and Juliet* (Festival, Chichester); *Pure Gold* (Soho); *No Boys Cricket Club, Party Girls* (Theatre Royal Stratford East); *Wuthering Heights* (Birmingham Rep); *Heartbreak House* (Watford Palace); *Sugar Dollies, Shakuntala* (Gate); *A River Sutra* (Three Mill Island Studios); *Rhinoceros* (UC Davies, California); *A Doll's House* (Young Vic).

She has previously been Associate Director of the Gate Theatre, Birmingham Rep and the Young Vic.

Richard Kent
Designer

For the Tricycle: *The Colby Sisters of Pittsburgh, Pennsylvania; Handbagged* (Tricycle/West End); *A Boy and His Soul; Paper Dolls.*

Current/Upcoming Work: *Bad Jews* (West End); *Man to Man* (Weston Studio); *Outside Mullingar* (Ustinov Bath).

Theatre includes: *Anything Goes* (Sheffield Crucible/UK tour); *This is my Family* (Sheffield/UK tour); *Bad Jews,* (Ustinov Bath); *The Merchant of Venice* (Singapore Repertory Theatre); *The El. Train* (Hoxton Hall); *Mrs Lowry and Son* (Trafalgar Studios 2); *Macbeth* (Sheffield Crucible); *Neighbors,* (HighTide Festival/Nuffield); *The Dance of Death* (Donmar at Trafalgar Studios); *Josephine Hart Poetry Week* (West End); *13* (NYMT, Apollo); *Clockwork* (HighTide Festival); *Titanic – Scenes from the British Wreck Commissioners Inquiry: 1912* (MAC, Belfast); *Richard II* (Donmar Warehouse); *Mixed Marriage* (Finborough); *Decline and Fall* (Old Red Lion); *Stronger and Pariah* (Arcola); *Gin and Tonic and Passing Trains* (Tramway, Glasgow).

Richard worked as Associate to Christopher Oram from 2008–2012 working on shows at the Donmar Warehouse, National Theatre, in the West End, on Broadway and at various International Opera houses.

Oliver Fenwick
Lighting Designer

For the Tricycle: *Red Velvet; Paper Dolls; Bracken Moor.*

Theatre includes: *Love's Labour's Lost, Much Ado About Nothing, Wendy and Peter Pan, The Winter's Tale, The Taming of the Shrew, Julius Caesar, The Drunks, The Grain Store* (RSC);*The Holy Rosenburgs, The Passion, Happy Now?* (National Theatre); *Routes, The Witness, Disconnect* (Royal Court); *Berenice, Huis Clos* (Donmar Warehouse); *My City, Ruined* (Almeida);

Di and Viv and Rose, Handbagged, The Importance of Being Earnest, Bakersfield Mist, The Madness of George III, Ghosts, Kean, The Solid Gold Cadillac, Secret Rapture (West End); *After Miss Julie* (Young Vic); *Saved, A Midsummer Night's Dream* (Lyric, Hammersmith); *To Kill a Mockingbird, Hobson's Choice, The Beggar's Opera* (Regent's Park); *Thérèse Raquin, The Big Meal, King Lear, Candida* (Bath); *Into the Woods, Sunday in the Park with George* (Châtelet, Paris); *The Kitchen Sink, The Contingency Plan, If There is I Haven't Found It Yet* (Bush); *A Number, Travels with My Aunt* (Menier Chocolate Factory); *Private Lives, The Giant, Glass Eels, Comfort Me With Apples* (Hampstead); *Restoration* (Headlong); *Hamlet, The Caretaker, The Comedy of Errors, Bird Calls, Iphigenia* (Sheffield Crucible).

Opera includes: *Werther* (Scottish Opera); *The Merry Widow* (Opera North/Sydney Opera House); *Samson et Delilah, Lohengrin, The Trojan Trilogy, The Nose, The Gentle Giant* (Royal Opera House).

Ben & Max Ringham
Sound Designers

Theatre includes: *The Ruling Class, Richard III* (Trafalgar Transformed); *The Walworth Farce* (Olympia, Dublin); *2071, Adler and Gibb* (Royal Court); *Minetti* (EIF); *Dawn French* (UK tour); *Fiction* (UK tour); *Blithe Spirit* (West End/US tour); *Boeing Boeing* (Sheffield Crucible); *I Can't Sing* (West End); *The Full Monty* (Sheffield/Noël Coward); *Jeeves and Wooster* (Duke of York's); *Ben Hur* (Watermill); *A Midsummer Night's Dream* (Michael Grandage Company); *The Pride* (Royal Court/Trafalgar Studios/UK tour); *Lungs* (Berlin Schaubühne), *The Hothouse* (Trafalgar Studios).

Ben and Max were nominated for a Best Sound Design Olivier for *Piaf* and *The Ladykillers* and as part of the creative team accepted a 'Best Overall Achievement in an Affiliate Theatre' Olivier award for *The Pride*. They won the Off West-End Best

Sound Designer Award in 2013 for *Ring* at the BAC.

They are associate artists with the Shunt collective and two-thirds of the band Superthriller. In 2013 they designed *Papa Sangre II* a sound-based IOS game for digital arts company Somethin' Else.

Harry Mackrill
Assistant Director

Harry is Resident Director at the Tricycle Theatre.

For the Tricycle: *The House That Will Not Stand; The Colby Sisters of Pittsburgh, Pennsylvania; Handbagged* (Associate/West End); *Red Velvet* (Tricycle/St Ann's Warehouse, New York).

Directing credits include: *This Isn't a Thing, Right?* (Nabokov Arts Club); *Coffee & Whisky* (Ovalhouse); *Look Back in Anger* (New Wimbledon Studio).

Richard Ryder
Accent and Dialect Coach

For the Tricycle: *The House That Will Not Stand; The Colby Sisters of Pittsburgh, Pennsylvania; Paper Dolls; Red Velvet.*

Richard Ryder has worked in the voice departments of the RSC and the National Theatre. He has just released an accent app for actors called 'The Accent Kit', a free download for iPhone and android.

Theatre includes: *Man, A Streetcar Named Desire* (Young Vic); *A Taste of Honey, Blurred Lines, Protest Song, 50 Years on Stage, Emil and the Detectives, Home, Romeo and Juliet, Untold Stories, Table, This House, Port, The Captain of Köpenick, Cocktail Sticks, Hymn* (National Theatre); *The Tempest, The Merchant of Venice* (RSC); *The Nether* (Royal Court); *American Psycho, The Turn of the Screw* (Almeida); *Fatal Attraction* (Theatre Royal Haymarket); *Fings Ain't What They Used To be, Oh! What a Lovely War* (Theatre Royal Stratford East); *Billy*

Liar, *Wonderful Town* (Royal Exchange, Manchester); *The Duck House, Uncle Vanya, King Charles III, Barking in Essex* (West End); *Race, Hysteria* (Hampstead); *Road to Mecca, In Skagway, Moby Dick, I cd only whisper* (Arcola); *Proof* (Menier Chocolate Factory); *Electra, The Winslow Boy* (Old Vic); *One Monkey Don't Stop No Show* (Eclipse); *The Thirty-Nine Steps* (Criterion/tour); *Anything Goes, Oliver, The History Boys, My Fair Lady, A Taste of Honey* (Sheffield); *The Kingdom* (Soho); *Beautiful Burnout* (Frantic Assembly); *A View From the Bridge, The Norman Conquests* (Liverpool Everyman); *Twist of Gold* (Polka); *It Just Stopped* (Orange Tree).

Television includes: *Crims, Amerikan Kanibal, Cradle to Grave, Apocalypse Slough.*

Film includes: *Set Fire to the Stars, Lady in the Van.*

www.thericthervoice.com
www.theaccentkit.com

Anna Cooper
Casting Director

For the Tricycle: *The Arabian Nights.*

As Casting Director:

Theatre includes: *A Number, Tonight at 8.30, The Saints, The Snow Queen* (Nuffield); *The Pitchfork Disney* (Arcola); *The David Hare season* (Sheffield Theatres); *Jeffrey Bernard is Unwell* (Theatre Royal Bath/tour); *Ghosts* (West End); *The Fastest Clock in the Universe, Lucky Seven* (Hampstead); *Educating Rita* (Watermill); *Measure for Measure* (Theatre Royal Plymouth/ tour); *Our Country's Good* (Liverpool Playhouse); *The HighTide Festival* (2007); *Scenes from an Execution* (Hackney Empire); *'Tis Pity She's a Whore* (Southwark Playhouse).

Film includes: *Act of Love, That Woman*

Radio includes: *Skyvers, The Reluctant Spy.*

As Casting Assistant:

Television includes: *Atlantis, Arthur & George, Silk, Doc Martin, Vicious, The Politician's Husband, Best of Men, George Gently VI, We'll Take Manhattan, Ashes to Ashes, Benidorm.*

Film includes: *The Lady in the Van, Belle, The Dark Knight Rises, Fast Girls, Ashes, SEX AND DRUGS AND ROCK 'N' ROLL, Poppy Shakespeare, Mr. Nobody, The Other Boleyn Girl, Angel.*

Theatre includes: *The Curious Incident of the Dog in the Night-time* (National Theatre); *Privates on Parade, Peter and Alice* (Michael Grandage Company); *The Real Thing, Six Degrees of Separation, Dancing at Lughnasa* (Old Vic); *A Delicate Balance, The Master Builder, Hedda Gabler, Festen, The Goat, or Who is Sylvia* (Almeida).

Lucy Hind
Movement Director

Lucy trained in choreography, mime and physical theatre at Rhodes University, South Africa, and went on to perform with the celebrated First Physical Theatre Company. She is Associate Director of the award-winning Slung Low theatre company and a selector for the National Student Drama Festival.

For the Tricycle: *The House That Will Not Stand.*

Theatre includes:

As Movement Director: *The Merchant of Venice* (Shakespeare's Globe); *Twelfth Night, The Sheffield Mysteries, This Is My Family, Love Your Soldiers, Playing for Time* (Sheffield Theatres); *The Jacobin* (Buxton Arts Festival); *Enjoy, Refugee Boy, The Wind in the Willows* (West Yorkshire Playhouse); *Manchester Sound: The Massacre* (Library); *Stuart: A Life Backwards* (Hightide/Edinburgh).

As a Dancer: *The Impending Storm* (DanceXchange/Unlimited Festival/Southbank Centre); *Boundless* (Dance Xchange).

As Dance Captain: London 2012 Paralympics Opening Ceremony (LOCOG).

Television includes: *Peter Pan* (BBC); *Banana* (E4/Red Productions).

Kevin McCurdy
Fight Director

For the Tricycle: *The House That Will Not Stand; Broken Glass.*

Theatre includes: *The Heart of Robin Hood* (world premiere, RSC/Dens Nationale Scene, Norway/Uppsala Stadsteater, Sweden); *Marat Sade, Twelfth Night, The Comedy of Errors, The Tempest, Julius Caesar, Much Ado About Nothing, Love's Labour's Lost* (RSC); *It's Not the End of the World, Cyrano de Bergerac, Suspension* (Bristol Old Vic); *We the People, The Frontline, Troillus and Cressida, Bedlam, Helen, Macbeth, The Comedy of Errors, King Lear* (UK/Middle East tour); *The Taming of the Shrew* (UK/Europe tour); *The Lightning Child, The Duchess of Malfi, The Knight of the Burning Pestle, Thomas Tallis, The Malcontent, The Changeling* (Shakespeare's Globe); *Batman Live World Arena Tour* (world premiere, O2 Arena); *Electra, Dream Story* (Gate); *Treasure Island, As You Like It* (Rose, Kingston); *Cause Célèbre* (Old Vic); *The Drowned Man* (world premiere, Temple Studios); *The Crucible* (Old Vic); *Miss Saigon* (world premiere, 25th-year celebration, West End); *The Story of Tom Jones* (world premiere, Dylan Thomas Theatre); *Bruises* (Royal Court); *Pomona* (UK premiere, Richard Burton, Wales/Gate); *Blisters* (Richard Burton, Wales/Gate); *Mogadishu* (UK premiere/Royal Exchange, Manchester); *The Last Days of Troy, Britannia Waves The Rules* (world premiere, Royal Exchange, Manchester); *Lotty's War* (UK premiere/tour); *Sweeney Todd* (Site Specific, London).

Film includes: *John Carter of Mars, Season of the Witch, Panic Button, Hunky Dory, Summer Scars, Berserkers, Set Fire to the Stars, The Lighthouse.*

Television includes: *Doctor Who Christmas Special, Torchwood, The Story of Tracy Beaker, Camelot, Pobol Y Cwm, Caerdydd, Alys, Switch, Hollyoaks, Hinterland, 35 Diwrnod, Stella.*

Opera includes: *Die Fledermaus, Il Trovatore, Rigoletto, Don Giovanni Woyzzeck, Die Fledermaus, Tristan und Isolde, Lulu, Carmen* (Welsh National Opera, Cardiff); *The Cunning Little Vixen* (Glyndebourne Opera House).

Emily Barratt
Costume Supervisor

Emily graduated from LIPA with a degree in Theatre and Performance Design and works as Wardrobe Supervisor for a theatrical costume hire store.

Theatre includes: *Titanic* (Southwark Playhouse); *The El Train* (Hoxton Hall); *Lizzie Siddal* (Arcola); *Cornelius* (Finborough).

As Costume Designer: *The Children* (Winchester Theatre Royal); *Twelfth Night* (Greenwich Playhouse).

SUPPORT US

The Tricycle is committed to bringing unheard voices into the mainstream and to presenting the world through different lenses – we are a place where cultures connect and creativity flourishes.

We need to raise at least £3million over the next three years to realise our ambitions to produce theatre that questions and entertains, support our work with young people in the local community, and transform the Tricycle in a major capital project.

The support we receive from charitable trusts, corporate partners and individual donors is more important than ever; please join us at this exciting time in the Tricycle's history.

With your support, we can continue to:

- create world-class theatre, like our Olivier award-winning production *Handbagged* and the critically acclaimed *Red Velvet*

- deliver over 22,000 Creative Learning experiences annually for young people in Brent and beyond to inspire a diverse new generation of theatre-makers and audiences

- transform the Tricycle into a welcoming space, with a more flexible, accessible and sustainable building in which to see and make theatre

JOIN US TODAY

Our members receive a wide range of benefits across stage and screen, with priority booking, invitations to member events, discounted theatre tickets, and opportunities to observe our Creative Learning work.

Membership starts from just £125 per year.

To join or for further details, please visit **www.tricycle.co.uk/support**, or telephone the Development Department on 020 7625 0132.

THANK YOU

We are extremely grateful to our supporters, whose help has made the work we produce at the Tricycle possible year after year. Thank you for your support.

PUBLIC FUNDING

TRUSTS AND FOUNDATIONS

INDIVIDUALS & CORPORATE PARTNERS

Major Donors
Jon and NoraLee Sedmak

Director's Circle
Christopher Bevan
Mary Clancy Hatch
Chris Hogg
Jeremy Lewison &
   Caroline Schuck

Pioneers
Liz Astaire
Jennie Bland
Kay Ellen Consolver
   & John Storkerson
Michael Farthing
   & Alison McLean
Gillian Frumkin
Judy Lever
Marjorie & Albert
   Scardino
Carol Sellars
Joseph & Sarah Zarfaty

Innovators
Nadhim Ahmed
Sue Allett
Henry Chu & James Baer
Claire Godwin
Tony & Melanie
   Henderson
Colette & Peter Levy
Andree Molyneux
Posgate Charitable
   Trust
Jackie Rothenberg
Rajeev Samaranayake
Professor Aubrey
   Sheiham

The Tricycle would also like to thank our Trailblazers and all anonymous donors.

We would also like to extend our thanks to our Big Give Christmas Challenge donors who are generously supporting Takeover 2015.

Cinema Box
Roda Fisher & Michael Hannaway
Bird & Alan Hovell
Anna Jansz
Ann & Gerard Kieran
John & Rose Lebor
M P Moran & Sons Ltd
Terry Munyard
Philip Saville
Glenis Scadding
Isabelle & Ivor Seddon
Barrie Tankel
Maggie Turp
Sandar Warshal & Family

Corporate Partners
The Clancy Group PLC
Casareccia
Daniel & Harris Solicitors
J. Leon & Company Ltd
JPC Law
London Walks Ltd
Mulberry House School

Opportunities for corporate partnership include production sponsorship, funding a creative learning workshop, or supporting another element of the Tricycle's work on stage or screen, with benefits for both the company and staff. Please contact the Development Department for further details.

CREATIVE LEARNING

Young People

The Tricycle has always been known for its work with young people. Since becoming Artistic Director, I have made this central to our mission. I didn't grow up being taken to see plays, but became involved by chance through a work experience placement in the local theatre. It changed my life. For me personally, it is vital that we offer inspirational opportunities that improve the lives of young people. Whether as audiences, writers, performers or producers of new work at the theatre, young people are at the Tricycle's heart.

Our Projects

Our work in the local community reaches out to marginalised young people. We work in mainstream and special needs education, with young asylum seekers and refugees and with children in some of Brent's – and the UK's – most deprived areas. The Tricycle helps give all these young people a voice, and the confidence to articulate it.

Tricycle Young Company offers 11–25 year olds the chance to make high quality theatre productions; developing skills, confidence and professionalism through work with the highest calibre artists. Their next Takeover will take place 22–29 March 2015, when over 300 young people will present live music, film and10 new theatre productions. If you want to know more about the learning activities and resources we have on offer, please contact us on

creativelearning@tricycle.co.uk or 020 7625 0134.

Indhu Rubasingham

Artistic Director

Story Lab

Plays for children, invented by children

The Tricycle's new literacy programme for primary schools began in autumn 2014. After a visit to the top secret Story Lab at the Tricycle, 321 children from local primary schools were given a challenge: to invent a story so brilliant and so original that storytelling would never be the same again! Their stories will be adapted for the stage and presented in a professional production: *Things Will Never Be The Same Again (and other stories)* 28 February–1 March2015.

Department for Education

SUPPORTED BY

MAYOR OF LONDON

FOR THE TRICYCLE

MULTITUDES

John Hollingworth

Acknowledgements

Thanks to Purni Morell and her (then) staff at the National Theatre Studio for their early support of the project – Sarah Nicholson, Gareth Machin and Matt Poxon.

I'm deeply grateful to all those in Bradford who took time to talk to me, especially Abdul Rehman, Bene and Hajra Amin, Liaquat Hussain and all at Jamiyat Tabligh-ul-Islam Mosque. Thanks to the New Muslims Project at the Islamic Cultural Centre at London Central Mosque, and especially to Jacqueline Kheir and to those whom I spoke with but who preferred not to be named. I'm also grateful to Signe and the girls at Mulberry School in Tower Hamlets.

Thanks to the myriad actors who did readings of the play in the past few years for their honesty and insights, and to Nick Cooper and Dr Conor McGrath for their invaluable help. This play wouldn't exist in the form it does without the generosity and hard work of the cast so deepest thanks to Clare, Navin, Salma, Maya, Asif and Jax for that and to Emma Tooze for policing the book.

I am indebted to Mike Bartlett, Caroline Steinbeis, Nic Wass and particularly Indhu Rubasingham for notes and guidance in developing the play. Thanks also to Jonathan Kinnersley and to all at Nick Hern Books.

Final thanks to Indhu for being a light to steer by in the darkness and to all at the Tricycle for their enthusiasm and unstinting support.

J.H.

For Anna and L.

'Do I contradict myself?
Very well then I contradict myself.
(I am large. I contain multitudes.)'

Walt Whitman, 'Song of Myself'

'Estimates vary as to the number of British converts to Islam in
the UK. Brice (2010) considers there to be somewhere around
100,000 British converts, calculated using data extrapolated
from the 2001 census. He also estimates that conversion is
occurring on a 2:1 ratio of females to males.'

Narratives of Conversion to Islam in Britain:
Female Perspectives
(Cambridge University Press)

Characters

NATALIE, *late thirties*
KASH, *forties*
QADIRA, *eighteen*
LYN, *sixties*
RUKHSANA, *leader of an Islamist cell, mid-thirties*
WAITRESS, *nineteen*
SISTER, *thirties*
SAM, *Deputy Political Director, Conservative Party, late
    twenties*
HARPREET, *eighteen*
MONICA, *in HR, late forties*
AMIR, *an imam, early thirties*
JULIAN, *Director of Conference Planning, CCHQ, mid-thirties*
IMTIAZ, *early twenties*
SHAFIQ, *mid-twenties*
SURGEON, *late forties*

*This play can be performed by as few as six actors or as many
as fifteen.*

Setting

*Bradford, September. Soon. The action (mostly) takes place over
six days.*

Author's Note

*The scene changes should be as fluid as possible and
unashamedly theatrical.*

Momentum is key.

Music would be good.

There may be no 'backstage'.

The scenes might overlap.

(…) indicates a failure or a reluctance to articulate

(?) indicates uncertainty

*(   ) indicates a refusal to speak that lasts the length of the
empty line*

(/) indicates the point at which the next character speaks

*(– .) indicates an abrupt termination or indication of a thing
unsaid*

[ ] indicates the unspoken completion of a thought

*This text went to press before the end of rehearsals and so may
differ slightly from the play as performed.*

ONE: FRIDAY, SATURDAY, SUNDAY

Friday

1. City Centre.

Night. AMIR *leads prayers in the City Park.*

2. Clock Tower.

It's chilly. It's late. KASH *in a suit and tie, smoking.* NATALIE *in work wear.*

KASH. If I had a megaphone I'd shout at them 'til their ears bled. Shout at them 'til they pack up and go. I'd just abseil down with it and –

NATALIE. You can't abseil, you.

KASH. How do you know?

NATALIE. Well can you?

KASH. Look at it.

NATALIE. They're tiny from up here.

KASH. It gets bigger every day.

NATALIE. They're brave. Women like that, out all weather.

KASH. They're using the car park as a toilet.

NATALIE. They're not.

KASH. They're showing me up.

NATALIE. Give us a go on that.

KASH. If you want one, have one.

NATALIE. I don't want one, I want a go on yours.

KASH. Can't you / just –

NATALIE. I'm doing you a *favour*.

She takes a drag.

Menthol?

KASH. Yeah. What?

NATALIE. What do you mean *what,* / like it's natural?

KASH. What were you doing?

NATALIE. Like it's alright. Like you work in *fashion*.

KASH. You looked like you were praying. When I came back up.

NATALIE. I dropped something.

KASH. So you knelt down and prayed for it?

NATALIE. Go on then.

KASH. What?

NATALIE. Give us a cig then.

KASH. No.

NATALIE. Don't be an idiot.

KASH. What did you drop?

NATALIE. What does it *matter*?

KASH. Why won't you tell me?

NATALIE. I just *dropped* something.

KASH. *What?*

NATALIE. A – coin.

KASH. A *coin*?

NATALIE. Why you being like / this?

KASH. Fifty pee? Twenty pee? / *What?*

NATALIE. I don't know!

KASH. How do you not know if you picked it up? You sort of scrambled up / when you heard me coming up the ladder.

NATALIE. No I didn't.

KASH. And then you pretended – badly – that you were picking something up.

NATALIE. What if I was praying?

KASH. So you were?

NATALIE. What does it *matter*?

KASH. ?

NATALIE. Yes! Okay, fine. Yes. I was watching them doing it down there. And – .

KASH. You decided you'd join in?

NATALIE. *Yes*.

KASH. …

NATALIE. What?

KASH. No. Nothing.

NATALIE. No come on / what?

KASH. Well it's a bit – .

NATALIE. ?

KASH. Why you acting like *I'm* the one being weird here? You're the one denying something you were *obviously* doing.

NATALIE. I'm not denying it.

KASH. Yeah but –

NATALIE. But what?

KASH. Okay.

NATALIE. *What?*

KASH. No. Nothing.

   Pause.

NATALIE. It's beautiful from up here. All of them standing with candles like that. The tents all lit up from inside. Like paper lanterns.

KASH *is unimpressed*.

What?

KASH. They're sitting ducks. Camped out in their *jilbabs* and *hijabs* like that. All it takes is some far-right farmer with a grudge and a shotgun / and –

NATALIE. You sound like the papers.

KASH. I expected some protests, after the General Election, after what the Tories said to win it. I knew they'd get some stick coming up here for conference but never *this*.

NATALIE. …

KASH. What?

NATALIE. You. Mr Westminster.

KASH. Hardly.

NATALIE. Getting your wig on.

KASH. 'Getting my wig on'?

NATALIE. It's a saying.

KASH. No it / isn't.

NATALIE. You're half talking to me and half doing your conference / speech.

KASH. I'm *not*.

NATALIE. I can see it in your / *eyes*.

KASH. It's a *massive* opportunity.

NATALIE. They only asked you cos the other guy wouldn't do it!

KASH. *Couldn't* do it. This is my chance to get some profile, some momentum to stand for Bradford West.

NATALIE. So why you so *wound* up / about it?

KASH. I'm *not*!

NATALIE. ?

KASH. I told them this shouldn't happen. It makes me look like an *idiot*.

NATALIE. How were you supposed to know?

KASH. I'm supposed to know everything, aren't I? *All* the brown thoughts. *Fifteen* years I've been a councillor. The city *finally* gets some attention and then *this* happens. And the worst bit is I'm going to have to *stand up* for that lot when I just wish they'd *go home*.

NATALIE. ?

KASH. *What?*

NATALIE. Nothing. You.

Beat.

KASH. Were you really praying?

NATALIE. Yeah.

KASH. Why?

NATALIE. ...

KASH. Nat –

NATALIE. I've got a surprise for you.

KASH. Have you got it with you?

NATALIE. It's a *surprise*. I'm not going to *tell* you.

KASH. Is it what I think it is?

NATALIE. ...

She's tender with him.

No.

3. Tent.

Night. RUKHSANA *in jilbab,* QADIRA, *frustrated.*

QADIRA. Could you not have got a better tent?

RUKHSANA. Better how?

QADIRA. Better than a children's one covered in pictures of Barney the purple dinosaur.

RUKHSANA. It's our Aisha's. What? She loves him.

QADIRA. *Guantanamo?* That's what they *used.* For sleep deprivation. Barney the fucking purple *dinosaur.* Spend more time plucking your eyebrows than watching the news, you. More time matching your headscarf with your mascara. Seriously.

RUKHSANA. I don't get time what with / our Aisha.

QADIRA. You look like the token woman on the make-up counter at Debenhams.

RUKHSANA. Nothing wrong with taking *care* of yourself.

QADIRA. What's that mean?

RUKHSANA. I'm just saying.

QADIRA. Just saying in my general direction?

RUKHSANA. What's up with you?

QADIRA. It's all I've heard all summer. All these attacks on mosques and all they *talk* about is what happened in *Coventry.* To *one* vicar. Are you even *listening* to me?

RUKHSANA. I've been cooking all day.

QADIRA. Course you have. Cos *that's* more important, isn't it? Food. Typical. There's always something more important than actually *doing* anything.

RUKHSANA. There's a revolution coming.

QADIRA. You're a female driving instructor. How is that revolutionary?

RUKHSANA. Look what they're doing over there!

QADIRA. Yeah! They're fighting for their lives against American troops while we sit in Greggs watching shit videos of it on your pay-as-you-go Samsung.

RUKHSANA. It's contract, yeah?

QADIRA. Oh well that's alright then, that makes all the difference.

RUKHSANA. Your dad pays your phone, doesn't he?

QADIRA. What if he does? What of it?

RUKHSANA. You're always *on* about him.

QADIRA. You're the one who brought him up!

RUKHSANA. At least I'm *here*.

QADIRA. As if it'll make a difference, this. Lezzing it off in / *tents*.

RUKHSANA. D'you ever wonder why I even *spoke* to you in the first place?

QADIRA. Spoke to *me*? *I* came over to your little *da'wah* table to ask what you were *up to* with your / little leaflets.

RUKHSANA. Yeah, you acted like you *owned* the / place.

QADIRA. Yeah cos my dad *built* that / mosque.

RUKHSANA. D'you think I'd have *bothered* with you if it wasn't for who your dad is?

QADIRA. / You don't *know* me.

RUKHSANA. D'you think I picked you for your brains? You're resitting your *A levels*.

QADIRA. / Yeah – because I – .

RUKHSANA. You'd *wet* yourself if someone popped a balloon in your ear.

QADIRA. / No I fucking wouldn't.

RUKHSANA. Got arms like twigs – you wouldn't last *two minutes* / over there.

QADIRA. I am fucking *ready*, yeah!

RUKHSANA. For what?

QADIRA. I'm not going to say it *here*, am I? We're in a fucking Barney the purple dinosaur tent! I want to *see* someone.

RUKHSANA. Who? Who do you / want to *see*?

QADIRA. *Whoever* it is that you *see* when you're *sick* of all this *talking*. Whoever *Nas* went to see. Whoever *that* is. I want to see *them*!

Beat.

RUKHSANA. Good.

QADIRA. ?

Pause.

RUKHSANA. It's a one-way thing though.

QADIRA. Fine by me.

RUKHSANA. You can't come back to us.

QADIRA. I can live without a *book group*.

RUKHSANA. Can you live without your dad?

QADIRA.

RUKHSANA. ?

QADIRA. *Course* I fucking can.

RUKHSANA. They'll text you, then.

QADIRA. Who will?

RUKHSANA. They will.

QADIRA. Who?

RUKHSANA. Whoever it is.

QADIRA. You don't even *know*?

RUKHSANA. That's how it works.

QADIRA. …

RUKHSANA. ?

QADIRA. *Fine*.

RUKHSANA. ?

QADIRA. *What?*

RUKHSANA. Did you bring the toilet paper?

QADIRA.

RUKHSANA. Oh *great*. That's brilliant, that is.

Saturday

4. Garden.

An hour after dawn, LYN *dressed smartly but pruning her roses with secateurs. She has iPhone headphones in and is listening to the radio on her phone. Some traffic.*

NATALIE. Mum.

LYN *is oblivious.* NATALIE *shouts.*

Mum!

LYN. Jesus!

NATALIE. / Sorry –

LYN. Where did you come / from?

NATALIE. There was no answer / so –

LYN. Frightened the *life* out of me.

NATALIE. Came round the / side.

LYN. Oh god. My –

LYN *taps her chest*.

NATALIE. Sorry.

LYN. No, no –

NATALIE. Are you alright?

LYN (*dismissive*). Yes yes yes – give me a moment – get these things off. So lovely to have Radio 4 *right* in the ears. Like they're stood right here with their feet in the flowerbed.

NATALIE. What you doing out here this early?

LYN *clicks off her phone*.

LYN. Oh I only came out to do the daisy bush but of course – the eye is *drawn*.

NATALIE. What have you done to the drive?

LYN. I mean it's a *riot* round this side. This lot are winter flowering but that lot's dead and I'm letting the Ceanothus just do its thing but the potting shed has gone a bit *Day of the Triffids*. Why didn't you say you were coming? I'd have done the cafetière.

NATALIE. Did you get my card?

LYN. Yes.

Beat.

Now – look – I'm rather late. I should be in a breakfast meeting with the manager at the hotel not massacring foliage and gassing.

NATALIE. I did go. I took some flowers down. Not that day, but –

LYN. Yes. You really shouldn't leave them with the cellophane on like that. It looks so sad when it rains. Anyway. It's the thought that counts. I took one of his joss sticks up. We had a little moment. Then a train thundered through, *as per*, and I had to get off. I mean – there's barely been a minute what with the conference lot arriving today and this bloody protest camp. I mean, it makes Bradford look *ungovernable*. What?

NATALIE. It's just – . Dad built the drive.

LYN. Well you weren't here to discuss it with.

NATALIE. Don't be like / that.

LYN. Every time I pulled the car up I saw him there laying the
flags. In his old pair of cords. Like it was yesterday. And I
just thought – oh come on Lyn it's been *five years*. And he
did a terrible job anyway. He was *awful* at anything practical.

NATALIE. And did it work?

LYN. It was a good distraction for a while. But no, it didn't.

Beat.

They bled him dry, that school. Take take take. If he'd
listened to me and retired when I asked him to then – .

Beat.

Anyway. Mustn't dwell. Kash hasn't forgotten we're
meeting tomorrow has he?

NATALIE. No.

LYN. Well tell him not to be late. And. Look. Natalie – .

NATALIE. What?

LYN. *Why* weren't you *there*?

NATALIE. I left you a message on the day.

LYN. You've never missed it before.

NATALIE. Look. You're always busy and –

LYN. That's hardly / *fair*.

NATALIE. I don't mean it like / *that*.

LYN. I haven't *seen* you for a *month*. Seen more of your –
'boyfriend' than / you.

NATALIE. I'm *sorry* I wasn't with you for the anniversary
but – . I'm doing something today and I'd like you to be there.

LYN. 'Doing' what?

NATALIE. It's at eleven o'clock. In town. I'll text you the address.

LYN. What is this thing?

NATALIE. Just – be there for me, will you?

LYN. But they're arriving this morning from *London* and I said I'd meet them and show them to the hotel and then go over His Lordship's speech for tomorrow night and I've got to get / my *hair* done!

NATALIE. Just. Please. Be – there. It would mean a lot.

LYN. …

NATALIE. Eleven o'clock.

LYN. I'll try.

NATALIE. I'll text you.

5. Bradford Interchange.

JULIAN *and* SAM *both wear well-cut suits, tote wheeled cases.* SAM *wears styled hijab.*

JULIAN. I thought it would be more *Asian*.

SAM. What does *that* mean?

JULIAN. 'Bradistan.' Tinsel. You know.

SAM. It's a bus station. What did you expect – elephants? What exactly does 'Asian' mean to you anyway? Do they *do* 'Asian' at boarding school?

JULIAN. I have *been*, you know. India. Elsewhere.

SAM. Pakistan?

JULIAN. No. Of course not, no one goes on a gap year to Pakistan.

SAM. I did.

JULIAN. Of course you did.

SAM. My parents are *from* there.

JULIAN. Of course they are. How old are you? What – sixteen, seventeen?

SAM. Twenty-seven.

JULIAN. Quite. And you went to, what, a comprehensive in a small market town? Mansfield? Didcot? Then – Oxford. Right? St Catherine's. Or the LSE if you didn't get the grades. You're the new breed. You're probably even religious.

SAM. I'm practising, yes.

JULIAN. Of course you are. You're authentic. You're a poster girl.

SAM. They said you'd be like this.

JULIAN. But you wouldn't be able to be you if I hadn't been me. Yeah? Three years I interned. Lived at home. Worked weekends in Gap. Before I even got a paid *job*. You're in the Party under two years and now you're the Deputy Political Director. So. You. This.

Gestures to hijab.

Progress. Good. But the wind didn't just *change*. It's thanks to people like *me* that you can be you.

SAM. You control the wind?

JULIAN. You can thank me later. Just don't forget you're junior to me.

SAM. Junior?

JULIAN. I outrank you.

SAM. It's not the *army*.

JULIAN. Yeah, it sort of *is* though.

SAM. *Okay chief.* Does it help if I call you that? *Chief?* You *wish* it was the army.

You're just the guy who gives out badges.

JULIAN. Passes.

SAM. Pen pots and paper clips.

JULIAN. And you've been over-promoted to within an inch of your life.

SAM. Because I'm brilliant / at my job.

JULIAN. You're charming and you're clever and you're not *bad* –

SAM. / 'Not – bad.'

JULIAN. But 'brilliant'? No. Fit? Perhaps. Good? Well – the jury's still out on that after you booked us all to come up here on the *National Express*.

SAM. It sends a message.

JULIAN. It says we've lost confidence in being ourselves. It's why we're standing in *Bradford* when we should be in Bournemouth or Buckinghamshire or the Brecon fucking Beacons or *anywhere else* beginning with 'B' where we could connect with our core vote.

SAM. Are you always like this?

JULIAN. I should have been a speechwriter.

SAM. You do know you ended up *sleeping* on me?

JULIAN. ?

SAM. This. Here.

She points to her jacket lapel.

That. Came out of your mouth. So…

JULIAN. What?

SAM. Looking is fine. Drooling is a bit much.

She produces rosettes, puts hers on.

Shall we?

JULIAN. *Here?*

SAM. I did say. Reaching out. All that. Did you not read the email?

JULIAN. Someone does that for me. You want to be careful with that on. They'd vote for a donkey in a red bonnet up here.

SAM. You're the one supposed to be 'engaging with the community'.

JULIAN. I am. I'm here, aren't I? I'm engaged. Look.

He takes the rosette and tries to put it on.

SAM. Good boy.

JULIAN. Fucking – . They never – . The thing's all –

SAM. Give it here. Come on.

She fixes it.

JULIAN. I'd have done it in the end.

SAM. Course you would.

JULIAN. Where's this woman? Where's our welcome? Come on *Bradford*. I'm ready to *engage*. It's always the 'B's. You'll learn this. When you grow up. Conference always has to be in a city beginning with 'B'. Brighton. Bournemouth. Birmingham –

SAM. Blackpool.

JULIAN. No. Not Blackpool. Blackpool's Labour.

SAM. 2007.

JULIAN. Yes of *course* 2007.

SAM. 2005. 1987. 1963. 1957. Shall I go on?

JULIAN. I *love* all the little facts you know. *Blackpool*.

SAM. We were in Manchester last year anyway / so –

    LYN *strides on*.

LYN. Excuse me – sorry – looking for Julian?

JULIAN. …

LYN. Is he with you?

JULIAN. ?

LYN. Julian? From Events and Visits?

JULIAN. Yes.

LYN. Oh.

JULIAN. What?

LYN. You're – ?

JULIAN. Lyn?

LYN. Yes! Sorry. LYN. L–Y–N. One 'N'. Yes! Forgive me.
Hello. *Hello*.

    SAM *extends her hand*.

SAM. Sam Qureshi. Short for Samara. We're *very* impressed
with the work you've been doing.

LYN. Oh.

JULIAN. The core vote really carried the election.

LYN. Oh. Well. We did what we could.

JULIAN. Your sort really saw us though.

LYN. My sort?

JULIAN. The spine. The *backbone*.

LYN. Oh. Well. Thank you.

SAM. It's *good to be here*.

LYN. Why ever did they send you up on the National Express?

JULIAN. Some terrible initiative taken by a child at Number 10.

SAM. It shows that we're not above travelling like most people do.

JULIAN. Except we are. I am / anyway.

SAM. I *love* this jacket.

LYN. I thought it might be going a bit too / far.

SAM. The PM would *love* it.

LYN. Would he really?

SAM. He *absolutely* would.

JULIAN. *Any-way*. So nice of you to meet and greet. Shall we go?

LYN. Of course. Forgive me. What am I like? Where are my manners? *Welcome to Bradford!*

6. Mosque.

NATALIE *now wears hijab. Everyone stands, expectant.* LYN *is close to* NATALIE. *Everyone's shoes are off.*

NATALIE. What?

LYN. Just – .

NATALIE. *What?*

LYN. You *know* what – [*this!*]

NATALIE. …

AMIR. Okay. Shall we – . You know. Yeah?

LYN. ?

KASH. Lyn – .

LYN.

KASH. Why don't you – come and stand here?

LYN *exhales loudly.*

She goes to stand near to KASH.

AMIR. Okay then. Right then. Shall we?

NATALIE *nods*.

Bismillah. 'I testify.'

NATALIE. 'I testify.'

AMIR. 'That there is no true God.'

NATALIE. 'That there is no true God.'

AMIR. 'But Allah.'

NATALIE. 'But Allah.'

AMIR. 'And that Muhammad, peace be upon him.'

NATALIE. 'And that Muhammad, peace be upon him.'

AMIR. 'Is the messenger of Allah.'

NATALIE. 'Is the messenger of Allah.'

AMIR. *Masha'Allah!*

LYN. Is that it?

NATALIE (*chides*). *Mum* –

AMIR. Not quite.

KASH (*calms*). Lyn…

LYN (*affronted*). Alright.

QADIRA *scoffs*.

AMIR. Shall we – ?

NATALIE *nods*.

'*Ash hadu Anla.*'

NATALIE. '*Ash hadu Anla*.'

AMIR. '*Ilaha Illa Allah*.'

NATALIE. '*Ilaha Illa Allah*.'

AMIR. '*Wa Ash hadu Anna*.'

NATALIE. '*Wa Ash hadu Anna*.'

AMIR. '*Muhammadan*.'

NATALIE. '*Muhammadan*.'

AMIR. '*Rasoolu Allah*.'

NATALIE. '*Rasoolu Allah*.'

   He smiles.

AMIR. *Subhan Allah!*

LYN. Is *that* it?

AMIR. Yes.

LYN. So we can go now?

KASH (*calm down*). Lyn –

LYN (*incredulous*). What?

   QADIRA *scoffs.*

KASH. Qadira –

QADIRA *What?*

KASH. Just – can the lot of you –

LYN. Did I say something?

NATALIE (*to* LYN). Just –

   She motions her to calm down.

LYN. What did I say?

   A moment.

AMIR. Okay. Right. Well done Natalie, yeah? Very well done.

QADIRA *scoffs*.

KASH. *Qadira* –

NATALIE. Kash – don't.

LYN. Look – shall we go? I think we should go. Come on – I'm going.

7. Fast Food.

A red-pleather banquette.

LYN. Well this really puts a ray of sunshine in the heart, doesn't it? I never even knew this place *existed*.

Beat.

Have you come far Amir?

AMIR. No. I'm from Bradford. West Bowling.

LYN. Were you at the grammar too?

AMIR. No.

LYN. Well I'm sure your school was just as good.

AMIR. It was in special measures.

LYN. Oh.

KASH. It was a faith school. Greenholme. You were in favour of closing it weren't you Lyn? You were quite proud, if I remember / rightly.

LYN. Kashif, I think – a day like today. We should – perhaps – *not*.

KASH. 'Not'?

LYN. For Natalie. Now – Amir. I had a question about the – 'liturgy' if I can – I mean I'm afraid I don't know your word for it, but – . Well – . I expected *more*, really.

AMIR. More…?

LYN. Not being – . You know. But –

AMIR. More… what?

LYN. I mean – I'm the crucifer.

AMIR. The whatifer?

LYN. I carry the processional cross at church and if there's an adult baptism we make it a part of the service. There's an excitement in the vestry beforehand and a celebration afterwards, everyone together for cake and a glass of red wine. Whereas that was – if I may say – a little *slight*.

AMIR. I see.

LYN. And I really don't mean / to be – .

AMIR. All you do to accept Islam is say your *shahada* in front of two believers and *understand* what it is that you're saying. Anyone can do it anywhere, at any time. That's the beauty of it.

LYN. Yes. I see.

> NATALIE *arrives with* QADIRA, *who slurps on a large Coke*.

NATALIE. They're bringing the drinks over and boxing the food up to make it easier to carry.

LYN. I thought we were eating here?

NATALIE. We are.

AMIR. Natalie wanted me to take some for the camp.

KASH. Did she?

NATALIE. Yeah. I –

AMIR. It's no trouble, I'm going down anyway for *salat*.

LYN. ?

AMIR. Prayer.

LYN. Thank you.

NATALIE. It's to celebrate.

LYN. Celebrate what?

NATALIE. Today.

LYN. Oh.

AMIR. It's *sadaqah*.

LYN. I'm sorry?

KASH. Charity.

LYN. So many new words.

> *A chippy, atonal* WAITRESS *arrives: ponytail, cap, hoop earrings, trainers.*

WAITRESS (*loud*). Lassis?

KASH. Yeah.

LYN. Excuse me?

WAITRESS. Three lassis?

LYN. Did we order those?

KASH. Yeah.

LYN. Do say 'yes' Kashif. I've never actually known what a lassi is.

WAITRESS. It's a lassi.

LYN. Yes but what actually *is* that?

WAITRESS. It's a yogurt drink.

LYN. Well surely it's either one or the other? Either a *yogurt* or a *drink*?

WAITRESS. Look. It's a lassi. Alright? Your food'll be five minutes.

LYN. Well I don't *have* five minutes. I've got to get back. Can't you – ?

WAITRESS *spins on her heel and goes*.

NATALIE. They're going as fast as they can.

    QADIRA *slurps her drink*.

KASH. Qadira don't.

LYN. Do Julian and Sam know you're feeding the camp?

NATALIE. Who are they?

KASH. The conference people.

QADIRA. This *stupid* conference.

LYN/KASH. Qadira!

KASH. I'm not feeding anyone.

LYN. You told the planning committee there'd be no trouble.

KASH. There hasn't been.

AMIR. It's a peace camp.

LYN. Oh *please*. You're just as against it as I am, Kash.

KASH. I never said that.

LYN. Oh, so you're *for* it now?

AMIR. ?

KASH. I thought we were – *not*. For Natalie.

LYN. Of course. I'm sorry. All a bit of a *shock*.

    Beat.

    QADIRA *slurps her drink*.

KASH. Qadira –

LYN (*to* KASH). Did you know?

KASH. Know what?

LYN. About today? Did she / tell you?

NATALIE. I can *hear* you.

KASH. Yeah.

LYN (*to* NATALIE). Why didn't you *tell* me?

NATALIE. You wouldn't have come.

LYN. You think that little of me?

NATALIE. You'd have been busy.

LYN. I couldn't find the way in. I was so *embarrassed*. The *looks* I got from people. My *heart* was going ten to the dozen. Could you not have given me any *warning*?

KASH. / Let's not –

LYN. I mean – *this* is what you've been doing? *This* is why you weren't there?

NATALIE. Yes.

   QADIRA *slurps her drink.*

LYN. Qadira. For *god's* sake. People are *gawping*.

KASH. Don't talk to her like that. / She's not –

NATALIE. Look – stop it the both of you. Please. Can we not just sit here as a family for once and *be nice*? One meal. Half an hour.

LYN. But I've got to / go.

NATALIE. Less than – okay? Let's just – . Sit. In peace. And eat. Our food. If it *ever* gets here.

   Long pause.

   QADIRA *slurps her drink. Everyone stares grimly at her.*

QADIRA. Whaaat?

8. Kitchen.

NATALIE *stowing cleaning things*.

NATALIE. Why you back so early?

KASH. Why didn't you tell me?

NATALIE. …

KASH. Nat –

NATALIE. I wanted it to be a surprise.

KASH. Yeah. Well. It was that.

NATALIE. I just wanted it to be us.

KASH. …

NATALIE. What?

KASH. Are you happy?

NATALIE. Do you know what *fitra* means? To be new-born, washed clean. No sin. No guilt. Happy doesn't cover it.

KASH. We should have done it properly.

NATALIE. We did.

KASH. …

NATALIE. Stood in the bathroom behind the main hall – washing myself, preparing myself – and then sitting on the little marble seats, rinsing my nostrils, washing my feet, I felt – . I've walked through that building so many times as an outsider looking in and – . I felt like I hadn't quite been *within* myself and suddenly –

She illustrates with her hands.

I was. I know that sounds – . And then Amir sang the *athan* and I felt the hairs on the back of my neck just – . And I *ran* down the corridor and into the back of the main hall and it was empty cos the men were using the side room and I just stopped *dead*. Had the place to myself. The sunlight through the stained-glass windows. The yellow of the dome. It was

so *peaceful*. I stood and I prayed and when I finished I felt
lighter, *different*. I *feel* different.

KASH (*carefully*). Do you want to get married?

NATALIE. What?

KASH. Is that what this is about?

NATALIE. No.

KASH. What, so you don't then?

NATALIE. No, but – why – are you *asking*?

KASH. ...

NATALIE. ?

KASH. Look –

NATALIE. Cos if you *are* it's not going well.

KASH. I know. At the start. You felt – . I know it took a year
before you moved in, but –

NATALIE. ?

KASH. Shit – you're right – this isn't going well.

NATALIE. ?

KASH. People *talk*. Yeah? You'd stop them breathing before
you'd stop them talking. Having a 'girlfriend' is one thing,
given I'm a... 'widower'. I mean I hate that *word* but – I
could *just about* get away with that. After Safia. People
gossip – yeah. But they mostly turn a blind eye. Let me get
on with my council work. But this. Now –

NATALIE. What?

KASH. Couldn't you have waited until the conference had
finished? Imtiaz is doing his nut! Says it looks like I've
converted you.

NATALIE. What's Imtiaz got to do with it?

KASH. / He's my adviser!

NATALIE. You only hired him because his dad works in / the restaurant.

KASH. *Manages* the restaurant *for* me. He could have come up with a – strategy.

NATALIE. It's not a *strategy*. It's my / life.

KASH. Why didn't you *tell* me?

NATALIE. I told you last / night!

KASH. Yeah and once I'd got it out of you there was no time to *talk* about it. I woke up and you were / gone.

NATALIE. I had to see Mum!

KASH. If I'm going to stand as an MP people will expect that we'll get married.

NATALIE. 'People.'

KASH. The community. They just will. So. Is that what you want? Eh? Is that what you were after?

Beat.

NATALIE. Well that is *definitely* the worst proposal ever. I mean – I don't have a lot of experience in the proposals department – I've only got one to compare it with but at least *he* had the decency to take me to Center Parcs before he asked me. At least he got down on one *knee*.

Beat.

I thought you'd be *happy* for me.

Beat.

For us.

Beat.

KASH. You should have *told* me.

9. Qadira's Bedroom.

QADIRA *trying on niqab, looking in a mirror.* NATALIE *enters with washing basket.*

NATALIE. Got any washing?

QADIRA. Can't you *knock*?

NATALIE. What you wearing that for?

QADIRA. Was that you *banging* about?

NATALIE. If you mean doing the washing up and putting it away then yeah.

QADIRA *scoffs.*

What?

QADIRA. Nothing. I'm thinking of wearing it.

NATALIE. Why?

QADIRA. Because I *am*.

NATALIE. Why didn't you come down for dinner?

QADIRA. I already *ate*.

NATALIE. Where?

QADIRA. Does it *matter*?

NATALIE. Did your dad not come up?

QADIRA. Why?

NATALIE. He said he would.

QADIRA. No.

NATALIE. He didn't speak to you? He didn't tell you to come down?

QADIRA. *No*.

NATALIE. Right.

QADIRA. What?

NATALIE. Typical.

QADIRA. Whatever.

NATALIE. Can you take that off when I'm talking to you?

QADIRA. Why?

NATALIE. Because I asked you to.

QADIRA. Why?

NATALIE. Qadira –

QADIRA. *Fine*.

> *She does. She indicates* NATALIE'*s scarf.*

> You've done that wrong, you know. The way you've pinned it. You don't need it on now anyway.

NATALIE. I know. I'm still getting used to it.

QADIRA. It should cover your chest.

NATALIE. Yes.

QADIRA. Your modesty.

NATALIE.

QADIRA. You shouldn't *decorate* it either. Like these girls today. Amir *never* tells them off. They're all bobbing backwards and forwards reciting and some of them have basically got *turbans* on. Like they might *tip over*.

NATALIE. You didn't used to wear one.

QADIRA. …

NATALIE. Your dad said.

QADIRA. He didn't want me to so I did.

NATALIE. Why didn't he want / you to?

QADIRA. Cos he's a *dick*. Cos he thought it'd 'hold me back'. That I'd get *judged*.

NATALIE. And were you?

QADIRA. By people who didn't matter to me, yeah. I was. So what?

NATALIE. Girls at school?

QADIRA. People use it as an excuse not to talk to you. It's like all this stuff in the papers about taking it off at airports, in court. 'Those poor women.' They haven't got a clue. They're glad really. They don't have to bother. You hate it anyway, right?

NATALIE. No. I don't.

QADIRA. You hate it when men won't look at you.

NATALIE. No.

QADIRA. It's what you're *used* to, right? 'S what happened with *Dad*.

NATALIE.

QADIRA. ?

NATALIE. It's alright to be scared, you know.

QADIRA. As *if*. Scared of *what*?

NATALIE. Boys.

QADIRA. What – you think I'm. WHAT?

NATALIE. I won't say anything.

QADIRA. About what?

NATALIE. You sneaking off.

QADIRA. *As if*. To where? Why would I even / – fucking –

NATALIE. I've said I won't say anything.

QADIRA. *Yeah* cos there's nothing to *say*.

NATALIE. One condition.

Text message beeps.

QADIRA. *What?*

NATALIE. Is that him?

QADIRA. *Who?*

NATALIE. Don't you want to know who it is?

QADIRA. Doesn't *matter* who it is.

NATALIE. You not going to check?

QADIRA. It'll be… Amir.

NATALIE. Course it will.

QADIRA. I'm *working* in the morning. Some *prayer* thing.

NATALIE. Yeah. Right.

QADIRA. I *am*.

NATALIE. ?

QADIRA. What condition?

NATALIE. Teach me how to do this properly.

QADIRA. Fine.

NATALIE. When?

QADIRA. Whenever.

NATALIE. Tomorrow.

QADIRA. Fine. Right. Night. Yeah?

NATALIE. ?

QADIRA. *What?*

NATALIE. You not got any washing?

QADIRA.

NATALIE. Night then.

   NATALIE *leaves.*

   QADIRA *checks the text: it's from* RUKHSANA's *contact.*

   A moment.

10. Kitchen.

LYN. I've run out of coffee. At the office. I didn't know where else to go. Everything is shut. Even the garages. I mean – . It's ludicrous. It's preposterous.

NATALIE. It's three o'clock in the morning!

LYN. Where's Kash?

NATALIE. In bed. You've got to stop with the coffee.

LYN. It's not the coffee. It's you. I checked the figures. The numbers. Conversions. Women up and down the country. Have you got anything to drink? Thousands every year. Did you know this? Have you or not?

NATALIE. How much have you *had*?

LYN. Every church is a *Mike's Carpets*! A bingo hall. An *Islamic Reading Room*. The poor vicars. They're *out* on their *ears* and no one says *anything*. Everyone's *terrified* to *offend*. But whilst we're all watching *Saturday Kitchen Live* and getting our bits from M&S and – yes – perhaps – *enjoying* a Campari and lemonade of an evening – there's an army of people out there – a *growing* army of people – shunning our lifestyle and *changing* the *fabric* of this *country*.

NATALIE. Don't be so / dramatic.

LYN. I mean. There were times in my year as Lady Mayoress when I'd have to do a speech. Open this. Open that. And the streets were *filthy*. The paint was *flaking*. And I couldn't say a word and I just wanted to *scream*. It was *gleaming* back then, Bradford. Steam trains. Gloss paint. Sandstone. *Civic pride*. Statues erected by public subscription to prominent figures, to politicians. Can you *imagine* that now?

NATALIE. / Not really.

LYN. A *statue* to a *politician*. I mean – it would be – what? An 'installation'. A six-foot-high pile of *dung* being stamped on by a giant mechanical foot, *again* and *again*. I mean. You

look at it now and it's *curdling*. It's *souring* like *off milk*
that's been *left* in the *sun*.

NATALIE. What is?

LYN. BRITISHNESS. And I mean – devolution. SCOTLAND!
Don't even get me *started* on Scotland. Those *bloody* – . The
whole country is – . I mean, have you *been* to the doctor's
lately? The one in Nab Wood? Every language under the sun
and which one do they put at the bottom, at the very foot?
The endnote? The *afterthought*? *English*. England – it's the
thing that's been trodden underfoot by the people *pouring*
into this country to get their grubby little hands on whatever
the Government will give them. All these Poles and
Lithuanians and Bulgarians and now *you*.

NATALIE. What?

LYN. You *join* them.

NATALIE. Join who?

LYN. *The other side*.

NATALIE. The other side? You're not a dowager countess! It's
not the *eighteen-hundreds*. England is your next-door
neighbour. It's whoever your kids are in school with. It's
messy and it's big and it's *many* and you can't print it on a
cake tin and / sell it at your coffee mornings.

LYN (*sharp*). Oh you're *just* like your dad. If it's foreign it's
better. The trinkets, the *travelling*, the *sandalwood carvings*.
It's a *fetish* for anything other than England. You just can't
admit it.

NATALIE. Look, I've said I'm sorry about missing Dad's
anniversary.

LYN. He'd be *ashamed* of you.

NATALIE. You mean you're ashamed of me. Go on. Say it. *Go
on*. I've embarrassed you. That's what you really think.
That's what you really came to say, isn't it?

LYN.

NATALIE. ?

LYN. If you don't have any coffee I should get back to the
office.

NATALIE. You're not driving like this.

LYN. I've a blouse in my desk.

NATALIE. You wouldn't get to the end of the road.

LYN. What do you care?

NATALIE. What's got *in to* you?

LYN. I'm just *worried* about you Natty – I'm *worried*! And – .

NATALIE. *What*?

Beat.

LYN. Nothing.

Beat.

I think I – . Might have. Over-poured that last Campari.

Beat.

Maybe you're right. Maybe I shouldn't – [*drive.*]

NATALIE. Sleep on the sofa.

LYN. ...

NATALIE. What?

LYN. Well. The others. The morning. I mean – [*I'll look a
state.*]

NATALIE. You'll be up and off before the rest of us like
always. You know you will.

LYN. ...

NATALIE. The words you're looking for are 'thank you'.

Sunday

11. Kitchen.

IMTIAZ *wears spectacles and a white hat. He's pedantic.*

NATALIE. Seriously? We're having a meeting about a *cake*?

KASH. Six cakes.

IMTIAZ. The cakes aren't the problem. The cakes look nice. The cakes look lovely. I'd quite like some cake actually. It's what you want to *do* with them that's the problem.

KASH. Sending food to the camp with Amir is one thing but going yourself – .

IMTIAZ. We have to think of how it could look.

KASH. I can't be seen to support them.

IMTIAZ. There's journalists everywhere. They're desperate for anything.

NATALIE. Who's going to care about me?

IMTIAZ. People know you. It could play very badly.

NATALIE. It's just cake.

IMTIAZ. It isn't just cake.

KASH. He knows what he's talking about, he's been a journalist / himself.

NATALIE. Right. Yeah. For who?

IMTIAZ. The *Keighley News* actually.

NATALIE. Oh. Right. / *Well then.*

KASH. And the *T&A.*

IMTIAZ. That was an internship actually. Photocopying and the like.

NATALIE. You're filling me with confidence.

IMTIAZ. Let me paint you a picture. You walk into the camp with a load of banana bread / and –

NATALIE. It's lemon drizzle cake.

IMTIAZ. I'm speaking metaphorically so that's not really important right now but – okay – you walk in with a load of – cake – and suddenly if the wind's blowing in the wrong direction the papers have got themselves a new poster girl for radicalism.

NATALIE. ?

IMTIAZ. The wrong picture at the wrong time can ruin everything.

NATALIE. This is about yesterday. You're punishing me for / yesterday.

IMTIAZ. Have you seen the Sunday papers? It's *all* Bradford. People are sick of reading about over there. Now the Americans are dealing with it they've stopped worrying about it. They're worrying about over here again. About another attack. Another Coventry if we send our troops in too.

KASH. Why d'you care so much about the camp now anyway?

NATALIE. / Because I *do*.

KASH. You didn't last week when the first tents / went up.

NATALIE. It's different now.

KASH. So you're in favour of what they're doing over / there?

NATALIE. They've stood up for themselves these women, they're not hiding themselves away, they're not afraid. All the stuff that gets said. They're being *brave*.

IMTIAZ. The point is this. There are twenty-seven non-white MPs in the House.

NATALIE. / Sorry?

IMTIAZ. There are six hundred and fifty sitting MPs.

KASH. Mate, I don't think now's / the time.

IMTIAZ. Now. I am a *fan* of mathematics.

NATALIE. / Oh my god.

IMTIAZ. Do you know what percentage of current MPs are non-white? Four point one five. Do you know what percentage of the population is non-white? Supposedly fourteen per cent but I have always had an instinctive distrust of whole numbers so it's almost certainly less – call it thirteen point nine eight per cent or maybe thirteen point / eight nine –

KASH. / Yeah – mate – we get it.

IMTIAZ. Anyway – there have only been *twenty-three* independent MPs in the last seventy years. Seventy years! There are only *eight* Muslim MPs at the moment.

NATALIE. What's your point?

IMTIAZ. If you want to increase the very low probability – and I mean that from a quantitative and not a qualitative standpoint – that you can achieve a majority and secure a seat at Westminster then every single vote counts.

NATALIE. You need an *adviser* to tell you that every vote counts? A media expert who worked for the *Keighley News*? Who did some photocopying at the *T&A*? Whose *dad* works in your restaurant?

IMTIAZ. *Manages* the restaurant.

NATALIE.

KASH. Mate. Look. Give us a minute would you?

IMTIAZ. Literally a minute / or –

KASH. Here – take this. Get down Greggs and I'll see you there, okay?

IMTIAZ *nods*.

IMTIAZ. Would it be alright to take a slice of cake?

KASH. No.

IMTIAZ. Okay.

He goes.

NATALIE. Wow.

KASH. I know.

NATALIE. ...

KASH. ?

NATALIE. The first time I saw you... You were standing in the middle of a crowd. In town. You were speaking about Syria. Why we *had* to go in. People hung on your every word. I didn't even know you. And I thought – who is *that*? Where's all that *passion* come from?

KASH. That was different.

NATALIE. No it wasn't.

She's tender with him.

You don't need some speccy kid to tell you what to / say.

KASH. The papers are out for blood. 'Them. That lot. The mass. The mob. The Muslims.' When's the last *positive* story you saw about Islam?

NATALIE. How about someone taking cake to / starving women?

KASH. When's the last time you saw the word 'Muslim' without the word, 'fanatic', 'extremist', 'radical' next to it? We're the enemy inside the gates. We're sexual predators, serial paedophiles. We're *mass-murderers* waiting for our moment to *strike*. They've made us the *enemy*. And once you create a credible enemy then you can do what you like to them.

NATALIE. Is that from your speech?

KASH. Think about how they could *use* it. How it could *look*.

NATALIE. I want to help those women.

KASH. Yeah?

Beat.

Then *don't go*.

12. Train Station.

A deserted platform. A large rucksack. A WOMAN *wearing dark jilbab and niqab. A stand-off.*

QADIRA. Are you going to say anything at all?

SISTER.

QADIRA. Right.

SISTER.

QADIRA. Is it a – ?

SISTER.

QADIRA. Is it?

SISTER.

QADIRA. Is this a test?

SISTER.

QADIRA. Do you know? If it is or it isn't? Or are you just the person who drops it off?

SISTER.

QADIRA. Okay. So maybe you put it together. Want to make sure it's used properly. Fair enough. But I'm not blowing myself up – no way – seriously – I never said I'd do that – that was never part of the plan so if you want me to do that then I'm sorry but you'll have to look elsewhere.

SISTER.

QADIRA. Look. I was just sick of talking. *Talking* and doing *nothing*.

SISTER.

QADIRA. This *is* a test isn't it? Whether I'm ready to put myself on the line. Whether I can *do* this.

SISTER. This isn't a 'test'.

QADIRA. What? *Shit*.

SISTER.

QADIRA. Look. Can I just go? I mean I haven't seen your face. Barely heard your *voice* and – . And I mean. Your skin looks. Sort of. Average colour. Not being – . But it's not like I could pick you out of a police line-up or anything. Not that I'd go to the police or anything. I wouldn't do *that*. It's just. I mean. D'you know what? My mum – died. Actually. Y'know? Bowel cancer. It's a few years now but – . Well I've been a bit – . Been quite – . I'm just a kid. That's what they said. The others – in the group. Said I wasn't ready. So can I just – go? Cos I'm actually. Quite scared. So – . If it's okay… I'll just –

SISTER. Open the bag.

QADIRA. Sorry?

SISTER. *Open* the *bag*.

QADIRA. Right. But – .

SISTER. ?

QADIRA. I mean it's not going to *do* anything, right? Not *here*. Not in *Pudsey train station*. You and me and a couple of *pigeons*.

   SISTER *steps towards her.*

   Right. Yep. Doing it now.

   Gingerly approaches the bag. Opens it.

   What – is that…?

   She explores it carefully. We don't see inside.

   What – is that *it*?

SISTER. We want you to burn it.

QADIRA. Burn it?

SISTER. We'll tell you where and we'll tell you when.

QADIRA. Right.

SISTER.

QADIRA. So, there's not a – ?

SISTER.

QADIRA. Well why didn't you say?... *Freaking me out!* I mean
– And it's just a – . I thought it was a – . And I was – . Sorry.
About – that. Before. I thought I had to – . But anyway. I
mean – this. Yeah. *This* I can cope with.

13. Shoe Rack.

It's empty except for two pairs of shoes next to each other.

NATALIE. Sorry? Do I know you?

SHAFIQ. Seen you 'round. You're new, yeah?

NATALIE. Not really.

SHAFIQ. You are, though.

NATALIE. I came before. To see Amir. To prepare.

SHAFIQ. Say your *shahada*, yeah? *Subhan Allah* – deep stuff.
How was it?

NATALIE. Yeah – good thanks.

SHAFIQ. *Masha'Allah* for that, sister.

NATALIE. Yeah.

SHAFIQ. *Masha'Allah* for that.

NATALIE. Thanks.

SHAFIQ. You can't have a dog though. It's *haram*. The saliva.

NATALIE. Yeah –

SHAFIQ. *Haram*.

NATALIE. I don't have a dog.

SHAFIQ. Paris Hilton has a dog. In her bag. A small dog. A lady's dog.

NATALIE. I'm not Paris Hilton.

SHAFIQ. Well – [*you are.*]

NATALIE. What?

SHAFIQ. You can't show your flesh neither.

NATALIE. No.

SHAFIQ. But she does. Always showin' off her flesh. Bikinis and stuff.

NATALIE. I'm not Paris Hilton.

SHAFIQ. All Western women are a little bit Paris Hilton.

NATALIE. What?

SHAFIQ. Nothing personal. 'S why I like 'em.

NATALIE. Are you *chatting me up*?

SHAFIQ. I'm just sayin'. I can protect you.

NATALIE. From what?

SHAFIQ. Y'know.

NATALIE. I don't.

SHAFIQ. Y'do though. Y'seen it. Them lot.

NATALIE. What lot?

SHAFIQ. Out there. Talkin'. Chattin'. The *buddees*. The *grandmas*. The aunties. Gossipin' about you and Kash.

NATALIE. ?

SHAFIQ. Oh yeah. Proper celebrities. Serious. I could protect you. Give you advice. You gotta play the game. You don't have any people, right? Any family. No one to recommend you.

NATALIE. Recommend me?

SHAFIQ. Talking *marriage*, yeah? Most girls say their *shahada* ten minutes before they say their *nikahs*, yeah? They're a single Muslim girl for ten minutes and then they're married. People know who they are then, how to treat them. But you – you're different now. You and Kash. People talking about it *enough* before. Him seeing some white girl, him being who he is. Not me, of course, but *now* people are *really* talking, you get me?

NATALIE. Right. What was your name?

SHAFIQ. Shafiq.

NATALIE. Okay, Shafiq. What I get up to with my partner behind closed doors is our business and our business alone but he's that concerned with what the community thinks that if he wants you to know something about us he'll probably flyer your street. And while we're at it *Shafiq* – your hair's a disgrace. Wash that gel out and sort your earrings out and ditch the sportswear and maybe *then* we can talk like we're *mates*.

SHAFIQ. You're one of us now, yeah? You got to watch yourself. Might find you need protecting sooner than you think.

NATALIE. Is that a threat?

SHAFIQ. No no. I'm telling you how it is.

NATALIE. …

SHAFIQ. You're welcome, sister. I'm around, yeah? Or you can bell me.

14. Hustlergate.

NATALIE *carrying her cakes from earlier.*

HARPREET. Will you though? *Please*. I only just made it out!
    They're fencing the whole camp in and my nappies are still
    in the tent. He's only there! In Greggs. I only need you to
    mind him for a minute. You can see the buggy in the
    window! Just while I get more nappies from Boots. It's all up
    his back and I don't want to move him and you lot always
    know what to do.

NATALIE. What d'you mean?

HARPREET. *Muslims*. Tonnes of brothers and sisters. Probably
    got a hundred kids yourself han't you, you're probably like
    forty-five or whatever and –

NATALIE. Harpreet –

HARPREET. How d'you know my *name*?

NATALIE. It's me. *Natalie*.

HARPREET. Who?

NATALIE. Miss Serjeant.

HARPREET. No *waay*! Oh my *god*! What you wearing *that* for
    then?

NATALIE. I – . Well, I've – .

HARPREET. No *fucking* way. That lad you're seeing made you
    do *that*? That is *well bad* / that is.

NATALIE. No one's made me *do* / anything.

HARPREET. That *grabbing* bastard. How dare he? He'll crate
    you up and ship you off before you can shout passport. Oh –
    for fuck's / *sake*.

NATALIE. What?

HARPREET. Manager's banging on window. ALRIGHT! He's
    like – the *last* man in the north of England what wears a
    toupee. I'M COMING YOU BASTARD! Can you help or
    not, miss? He's proper *fountained* front and back.

NATALIE. Can't you ring your / mum?

HARPREET. She'll just go *on* at me like she *always* does and
anyway we're not speaking at the minute cos I wouldn't give
him a Sikh name and then I kept getting caught with him in
school.

NATALIE. So you did go back then?

HARPREET. College, yeah, *course*. They encouraged it. Life
skills and that. Like, attachment parenting. Did a module on
it. But sometimes I'd just take him in the backpack.

NATALIE. In a backpack?

HARPREET. I'd leave the *zip* open. *Anyway*. Last week I'd had
enough so I just walked out with the buggy and moved into
the camp. Had Haylee changed by like a million different
women and it was well good and then they came this
morning and started fencing it in.

NATALIE. Who did?

HARPREET. This *fucking* conference. I can't *believe* they'd
show their face up here, me, after what they said during that
election. All them sign boards going round with 'Who's
Britain Is It?' All that stuff about immigrants. They've got
some *proper* cheek.

NATALIE. You called him Haylee?

HARPREET. Yeah with two 'E's. Like in the film, like 'I see
dead people.'

NATALIE. ?

HARPREET. That *film*. The kid with the face. It came out like a
million years ago. 'I see dead people.' Look – mind Haylee
for two minutes and the manager'll stop being a dickhead
and you can give me a hand changing him and everything'll
be alright and we can put your boxes in the buggy after and
wheel them over to the camp and everyone's a winner, yeah?
That's where you're going with that lot, right?

NATALIE. You said it was fenced off.

HARPREET. *Honestly* didn't you learn *anything* teaching me? There's a back way. By the Chinese. There's *always* a back way.

NATALIE. ...

HARPREET. You'll be *brilliant*! All the Muslim girls in college were like all natural-born mothers or whatever – like all clean hair and nice nails and he'd go quiet as soon as they picked him up. Miss. Honestly. You'll be *amazing*.

NATALIE. ...

HARPREET. Pleeeeease?

15. Hotel.

A scuffed tea trolley with sorry-looking tea service. KASH has a manila envelope.

LYN. I *asked* for the *platinum* tea service and *specifically* requested Assam tea and their *best* china so I *cannot fathom* why the manager would leave *this* out unless he *meant* it as some sort of *open insult* to the Party.

JULIAN. The tea's not the / problem.

LYN. There isn't even a *spoon* for the *sugar*. I'll have his *guts* for *garters*.

SAM. You're *absolutely* right. Would you mind having a word?

LYN. Well, I *had* hoped I'd hear some of Kash's / speech.

SAM. We'd be *ever* so grateful. Wouldn't we?

JULIAN. Absolutely.

LYN. Oh. Well. Yes, alright then. I shan't be long.

She nods, leaves.

JULIAN. As you were *trying* to / say –

KASH. *Whose* idea was the *fence*?

JULIAN. None of us are happy about this.

KASH. I didn't get a call.

JULIAN. It makes us look heavy-handed.

KASH. I normally get a call.

JULIAN. It seems to be the contractors' initiative.

SAM. They say it came from you.

JULIAN. Well it wasn't 'me' me.

SAM. Yes but it came from your *department*.

KASH. From who?

SAM. Events and Visits.

KASH. I'm lost.

SAM. He's conference, I'm strategy.

JULIAN. I make things happen, she tells people what to do.

KASH. And the fence?

JULIAN. Well – it wasn't *me*.

KASH. Well it's there, isn't it, I mean look at it. It's *there*.

JULIAN. No one's saying it isn't there.

SAM. Kash – we came here to build bridges, not fences.

> JULIAN *gives* SAM *a look.*

> I'm sorry you didn't get a call.

KASH. Yeah. I don't mean to be – . But –

SAM. No. You're quite right. It's a shock for all of us.

JULIAN. I may as well have slept in a phone box last night the
     number of *calls* I took.

KASH. You've not been up here before have you?

JULIAN. No.

KASH. It's – difficult out there.

SAM. We're well aware of that.

KASH. After the mosque attacks – people are on edge.

SAM. That's why we're here. That's why you're here.

JULIAN. The Party is – *wary* of engaging in the wrong way.

KASH. Like building a fence around a peace camp?

SAM. We've got it wrong before.

KASH. You can say that again.

SAM. We know we need to engage. We know the coalition made mistakes.

JULIAN. But we never expected this. It looks like Glastonbury gone wrong.

SAM. Is that the speech?

KASH. Yeah.

JULIAN. Printed. Old school. I like it.

KASH. My adviser's emailed a copy.

SAM. Can you give us the bullet points? We're pushed for time.

JULIAN. He could read it.

SAM. He'd have to read it *quickly*.

KASH. People are scared.

JULIAN. Sorry, have you started? Is this *it*?

KASH. No.

JULIAN. Oh. I thought that was a strong start.

KASH. Well – I do *say* that. Look. Why don't you just read it?

JULIAN. Someone does that for us.

SAM. We just need the overview.

KASH. This is the problem. Everything has to be shorthand. Quick fixes. The *overview* is that it's fucking complicated to rebuild trust.

JULIAN. Well, I mean, the sentiment's good but the *swearing* – .

SAM. Not so good.

KASH. I'm not going to swear, am I? That was just – me talking.

SAM. 'Rebuilding trust', I like. That's on-message. You know – 'we're better together.'

KASH. Those women down there don't want another war. They don't want more Muslim casualties. They don't want this country being dictated to by America again and again and again.

JULIAN. That's *less* on-message.

SAM. That's off-message actually.

KASH. Forget it. Just read it and…

    KASH *sees something*.

JULIAN. What?

KASH. Did you see that?

SAM. See what?

KASH. Down there.

SAM. Where?

KASH. *Right there*. By the forklift with the fence panels.

JULIAN. Some sort of scuffle.

KASH. The security guys just pushed that girl over.

JULIAN. They don't just 'push people over'.

SAM. I'm sure they were just *manoeuvring* her.

JULIAN. They're trained professionals.

KASH. They *pushed* her.

JULIAN. Or did she fall?

KASH. Are you serious?

SAM. I didn't see it.

JULIAN. What was the *nature* of the *contact*?

KASH. The nature of it?

JULIAN. Because, not being – . But –

KASH. What?

JULIAN. Well if she *came* at them and *fell* then –

KASH. She didn't '*fall*'.

    JULIAN*'s and* SAM*'s phones ring: standard tones.*

    A moment.

JULIAN. I'm sure it's nothing.

SAM. This happens all the time.

JULIAN. Ministers fighting over the running order.

SAM. Local Party wanting in on the act.

KASH. You not going to answer?

    A look between SAM *and* JULIAN.

    Beat.

Because she's not getting up.

16. Kitchen.

QADIRA *on her phone,* NATALIE *has a pillar candle,* LYN *has a bottle of wine in hand.*

LYN. She shouldn't have resisted being moved on!

KASH. Lyn – she's in a coma.

QADIRA. Have you *seen* it?

LYN. How is *burning* a *candle* supposed to help anyway?

QADIRA. They're *shoving* her, / you can see them!

LYN. It was very brave of Joseph to say there was a problem. / We didn't rehearse that.

KASH. I thought you didn't like him?

LYN. Oh *god.* I *don't.* He wants my job as party chairman and he's a lucky sod.

NATALIE. Why?

LYN. Well it's hardly a *coincidence*, him being Lord Mayor this year, is it? Joseph *Ayebe.* And no – come on – before / you all start – it's *not.*

NATALIE. You shouldn't *say* things like that.

LYN. Oh don't be so *dour* Natty. The drinks reception was *terrible.*

KASH. You did well out of it.

Indicates her bottle of wine.

NATALIE. Yeah – I think. Mum. Shall I – take that / now?

LYN. Honestly. The service was so *slow. / The faces* on those girls serving.

NATALIE. Why don't you give it to me?

LYN. Like *slapped fish.* Are you going to / light it or what?

NATALIE. It's not time.

LYN. Silly / idea anyway.

NATALIE. I think a vigil is a very moving gesture.

LYN. You would. You *sure* it isn't / time yet?

NATALIE. / Not for another *minute*.

LYN. Qadira put your *phone* away.

QADIRA. You can *see* the security guy *shove* her. / They killed her for nothing!

LYN. She should have gone when she was *asked*, / now *put it away*.

QADIRA. She wasn't 'asked' / she was –

LYN. How was the food?

NATALIE. I didn't have any, it wasn't *halal*.

LYN. Well why *should* it be? / Now do we sit or stand or what?

NATALIE. What's got *in to* you tonight?

LYN. Where do you want me?

QADIRA. Stupid idea anyway.

LYN. For once / I couldn't agree more.

KASH. Look – both of you – / *leave* it.

NATALIE. It's not *just* about that woman.

QADIRA. She has a *name* you know.

LYN. / Don't we *just*!

NATALIE. It's not just about Shirza.

LYN. / All we'll hear about.

NATALIE. It's about *every* life that's been affected.

LYN. / Oh *please* don't start *this*.

NATALIE. Whether / it's Coventry or a drone strike or whatever.

LYN. They were *doing their job* and she *banged her head*, / it was her *own fault*.

KASH. They pushed her Lyn, / it's *clear as day*!

NATALIE. Alright! Alright. *Alright*. It's time.

> *They fall silent.*
>
> *She lights the candle.*
>
> *Thirty seconds pass.*
>
> LYN *swigs from the bottle.*

KASH. Lyn –

LYN. You didn't / give me a glass.

KASH. Can you not?

LYN. *What*? / Honestly –

QADIRA. I'm not / keeping quiet if she's not.

NATALIE (*to* LYN). / Look what you've done now.

QADIRA. You didn't even *ask* if you could *drink* that / in here.

LYN. I've *never* had to ask *before*.

QADIRA. It's *haram*!

LYN. Well you should have *said* / if it's a problem.

QADIRA. We're saying *now*!

KASH. You stay out of it. / You should have *thought*.

LYN. Well I'm *sorry* if I've broken a *rule* that / I didn't even *know* about.

QADIRA. Get it off her.

NATALIE. 'Get it off her'?

LYN. Get it off *who* – / the cat's *mother*?

KASH. Give it to me. / Come on –

LYN. / No!

> *A scuffle.* LYN *is relieved of the bottle.*

NATALIE. There's no need to do / *that*.

LYN. Well I / *never*, I –

NATALIE. Lyn –

LYN. Give. That. Back. Right. / Now!

NATALIE. You've had enough.

LYN. I'll *say* when I've had *enough* you / load of *nannies*.

NATALIE. You're drinking too much since Dad died.

LYN. I don't need to *ask* permission from *you* / if I want to *do* something.

NATALIE. Mum you *are*. / You need to –

LYN. *I* don't have to do *what you* / *tell me*.

KASH. You do if it's in our *house*.

QADIRA. / Yeah!

LYN. Jesus *Christ*! Oh *that* is *typical*. All this *rigmarole* / and *folderol*.

NATALIE. / It's not *rigmarole*.

LYN. Shake hands, don't shake hands. *This* is *haram*, *that's haram*. You *can* say this, you *can't* say *that*. And now I can't even have a drink in my own daughter's / *house*!

KASH. Yeah – not without / *asking*.

LYN (*to* KASH). *You* don't tell *me* what to do. This is *my bloody country*!

NATALIE. / Don't start *this*.

LYN. Do you know who the happiest people in the world are? THE SCANDINAVIANS!

NATALIE. / Oh here we go. Here it comes.

LYN. Do you know why? Because they're *homogenous*. *Everything's* the *same* – the houses, the cars, the hills, the fjords, the hair, the skin, *the DNA*. It's *all* the *same*.

NATALIE. / Exactly! It's *shit*.

LYN. The very *stones* of the place, the fabric of the community, generation upon generation who've lived together / with a shared *purpose* and a shared *language*.

NATALIE. You've never even *been* to Scandinavia!

LYN. I mean *I* don't go abroad and demand roast beef and Yorkshire pudding / with everything do I?

NATALIE. / You don't *go* abroad!

LYN. No! I smile and I say thank you, *whatever* I'm brought, because I'm *British*.

QADIRA. / *Yeah, we got that.*

LYN. Because I know that *abroad* is a country where things are done differently and if you don't *like* that then you don't *go* there.

KASH. / Who are you talking to?

LYN. If you have to have everything done *your* way, if you want to have everyone show *respect* for who you are and how you live your life then *stay where you are.*

KASH. / Are you saying this to me?

LYN. And if you *do* go abroad then you pack your bags full of courtesy and you learn the words for please and thank you and you show respect for the way things are done in that place / and if you don't *like* that –

KASH. / Is this for me?

LYN. If you don't like your girls going to school, if you don't like your women to be looked at, if you don't like your kids to be educated outside of their faith –

NATALIE. / Oh my god.

LYN. If you want them to speak Urdu, or Kashmiri, or Punjabi or *Polish* / for that matter – before they speak English –

NATALIE. / Yeah, insult *everyone*, you may as well.

LYN. Then it sounds like you'd be happier if you took them with you and you went back *home*.

Beat.

KASH. You've held that in for years haven't you?

LYN. What if I *have*?

KASH. You *enjoyed* that. / The *look* on her face!

NATALIE. Don't, there's no point when she's like this.

QADIRA. I get shouted at by builders, by total strangers –

NATALIE. / Oh don't you start. That's all we bloody need.

QADIRA. By people who should know *better*. I'd *love* to live somewhere I'm not an *outsider*. Where I don't get stared at on the bus. The little comments, the looks –

LYN. So go home then!

NATALIE/QADIRA. / *What?*

KASH. You can get out if / you're going to talk like that.

NATALIE. / No Kash just *leave* her alone, the state she's in.

QADIRA. Where's *that*? What other home have I *got* apart from *this*? This is what they set up *over there*. A home for all Muslims. A caliphate.

KASH. / It was a rogue state, a bunch of *bandits*.

QADIRA. But no – *America* says no and they send their troops in and now Britain will end up going / in too.

KASH. It's a war on *extremism*. On Muslims who kill / Muslims.

QADIRA. I was watching this – I saw this kid *disappear*, okay? / He got hit by an American tank –

KASH. / Where did you see that?

QADIRA. For *throwing rocks*. And they just / *disappeared* him into red mist.

LYN. I think he was probably doing more than / *throwing rocks*.

QADIRA. They *killed* him cos they *could*. He was just some *goatherd*.

LYN. I'm sure he was *dressed* as a / goatherd.

QADIRA. All he had on was a *dhoti*!

LYN. He probably had an AK47 under it. *That's* what we're *up against*!

NATALIE. W*hat's* what you're up against?

LYN. Kids with guns. *Marauding* attacks. / The fight on our doorsteps.

KASH. / Oh *please*, this – .

LYN. This *constant* threat.

KASH. And what *is* that threat?

LYN. What do you mean?

KASH. You don't know the difference between Wahhabis –

QADIRA (*correcting*). / Salafis.

KASH. And Deobandis and Barelvis or Twelvers and Ismailis and Fivers.

LYN. / No I don't, why *should* I?

KASH. We're all just a big *threat* to you, even the Sufis, even the *nice guys*, we're still just a bunch of *Muslims*. Just one big *enemy*.

LYN. Well *that's how it feels*.

NATALIE. / Oh my god!

KASH. But *that's not how it is*. Your enemy is my enemy.

LYN. / What does *that* mean?

KASH. Terrorism in the name of Islam. *Anyone* who says you can force people to convert, that it's alright to use violence, to use terror, to blow people up. / They are *our* enemy.

QADIRA. Yeah but –

KASH. No buts –

QADIRA. If we're at war –

KASH. We're not at war.

QADIRA. The West's been at war with Islam my entire *life*!

LYN. / 'The West'?

QADIRA. The Gulf *War*. The UN *standing by* during Srebrenica.

KASH. / Standing by isn't war.

QADIRA. Bush and Blair's Iraq. Then Afghanistan. Now America sending troops in over there – year upon year of *aggression* against Muslim states!

KASH. / Who taught you that?

QADIRA. Of *course* we're fighting back! *Finally*.

KASH. / 'We'? Who's 'we'?

QADIRA. It says in the *Qur'an* that fighting is laid down for us, even if we don't like it.

KASH. / Yeah but the *context* of that is –

QADIRA. It doesn't *matter* if you don't like what they're trying to do over there – it's a *revolution*. They were trying to bring all Muslims together.

KASH. / Qadira, they weren't.

QADIRA. To *unite* the *Ummah*. You lot make me laugh, scratching your heads when the next teenager goes over there to help.

LYN. / It's not *funny*.

QADIRA. *What* is so *hard* to understand about that when the alternative is being *grateful* to be *tolerated*?

KASH. / You sound like Nas did.

QADIRA. What – they should stay for *that*? Yeah *right*. The
news is all like – '*who* would go over there', 'how *could*
they?'

LYN. / And how *could* they?

QADIRA. They're the girls in *hijab* you keep *staring* at on the
bus! The lads you picked on in school for not going
swimming. The women in *niqab* you're *muttering* about and
shouting at in the street.

LYN. / I don't do that. I'd *never* do that.

QADIRA. The next young Muslim you treat like shit is the next
young Muslim on a plane over there.

LYN. / Oh you're as *naive* as they are.

QADIRA. And the only thing that's *radical* about them is that
they managed to stay *patient* for so *long* so don't *patronise*
them!

KASH. They're being taken advantage of.

QADIRA. You tell yourself that because it's easier to believe
than the truth.

KASH. Which is what?

QADIRA. That they can't *wait* to go.

LYN. / I can't believe that *at all*.

QADIRA. They can't *wait* to do something that actually makes
a *difference*. *That's* why Nas went. Don't say you 'can't
believe it' – it's how the world *works*. You want something,
you take it. Look at Russia with the Ukraine –

LYN. / That's a good example is it, Russia?

QADIRA. China with Tibet then! What did your cherished
British Empire do then, eh? If it *wanted* a country, it *took* it
and if you got in the *way* then you were *dead*. I'm not
British.

LYN. You were *born* here!

QADIRA. / That's not *my* fault!

LYN. This country *raised* you, it *fed* you, it *educated* you and after all *that* you say it doesn't *matter* / to you?

QADIRA. It doesn't matter. I'm not *British*.

KASH. Then what / are you?

QADIRA. I'm Muslim. What are you?

KASH. British – obviously.

QADIRA/LYN. / No you're not.

NATALIE. Mum. / Don't.

KASH. *What?*

NATALIE. Wait a minute / all of you.

LYN. You weren't *born* here.

KASH. I came here when I was *one*. This is my country.

LYN. Kash – come on – it isn't. Not really.

NATALIE. / Stop this. Now!

LYN. Not deep down. It's not! What's so *wrong* with *saying* that?

KASH. / This is my country.

LYN. Kash – come off it. All you ever *talked about* in the council chamber was 'the *problem* with / this country'.

KASH. Yeah the *problem* with this country is people like you!

NATALIE. Kash, don't, please.

KASH. People *flock* to this country because of what it *stands* for and for the chance to live in a *decent* society and honour the country you came from.

LYN. / That doesn't *work*! It's *one* or the *other*!

KASH. This country's being *ruined* by people like *you* not the *immigrants* you keep going on about. Who delivers front-line

NHS services? Who's propping up the British Army? Lads from up the Buttershaw Estate? It's Gurkhas, Fijians, Samoans. Who's taxiing your kids to school in a morning?

LYN. / I haven't taken a taxi since *Rotherham*.

KASH. Driving you home at night after your Campari and lemonade, eh? Who's selling you your milk for the morning in the middle of the night? Who's building your houses for cash?

LYN. / I never employ *those* people.

KASH. Who'll be digging your grave *by hand* with a *spade* because that's beneath the dignity of the British working man? IMMIGRANTS! My dad came here from Pakistan and got a job in the first mill he walked into on the first day he got here and he got that job because that company *needed* him and that company *gave* him that job because *they needed* to make a profit and pay their taxes and those *taxes* paid for school places for his children and mine, for his health care and mine, so don't talk to me about charity and handouts.

LYN. / I didn't. I never said *you* took handouts. I didn't mean *you*.

KASH. Because my dad *loved* Britain. He *loved* it. He'd smack us round the ear for dropping litter.

LYN. / Well good for him!

KASH. He sang the national anthem. He videoed the Queen's speech. He lived through partition, through the carving up of his country by this one, and *still* he loved Britain. Worked his whole life here. Bought his house. Raised his kids and why has he gone back to Pakistan? Because he said he didn't *recognise* this country any more and it broke his *fucking* heart!

LYN. Then your dad was a model citizen! It's your *daughter* that's the problem.

QADIRA. / I'm not a *problem*.

LYN. It's your daughter who wants to *go*.

QADIRA. D'you blame me with all *this* shit going on? D'you think I feel safe? You can keep your bags full of courtesy and respect. You can *have* Scandinavia. You can keep your crappy Royals and your crappy little island and / you can fucking *rot*.

NATALIE. That's *enough* Qadira.

LYN. Oh. *Natty* – come *off* it.

NATALIE. / Off what?

LYN. You're part of the problem too – you're *desperate* to be *anything*, to be *anybody* other than who you *are*.

NATALIE. / Don't start on me now you're on a roll.

LYN. These *endless* causes and spiritual *journeys*! Your Buddhism. Your travelling. / Your little *tattoo*.

NATALIE. That was *years* ago!

LYN. You're in *flight* from yourself. You've never *known* who you really *are*.

NATALIE (*venom*). / What?

LYN. Well you haven't. You absorb whatever's around you. You're like a bloody *sponge*. That's all this whole *thing* with / Islam is.

NATALIE. It's not a *thing*.

LYN (*driving on*). Oh *come on*. You're being *ridiculous*.

NATALIE. / Can you not respect what I've done for once? For *once* can it be good enough? Can't you just say you're happy for me?

LYN. *Everybody* thinks so. I'm only saying what everyone else is thinking. This whole happy-clappy hippy-dippy love-in is a *fantasy*. The multicultural project doesn't *work*!

NATALIE. / Yes it does, of *course* it does.

LYN. It's never *worked*. We just *pretend* that it does. But *really*, what we *really* want if we're honest with each other is for everybody else to be like *we* are. People living with people from different places – it's a by-product of the jobs market! It's an *accident*.

KASH. / An accident. I'm an *accident*?

LYN. We don't have to *celebrate* that. We don't have to *like* it. And people *don't*.

NATALIE. / They do.

LYN. Birds of a feather flock together.

NATALIE. / What does that even *mean*?

LYN. It's why people go on *cruises*!

NATALIE. / Oh my god. *Cruises?*

LYN. I mean look at Bradford! The immigration from Pakistan. I'm told it's *tribal*.

KASH. / '*Tribal*'? Oh that is – . *Tribal?*

LYN. Mirpuris over here, Kashmiris over there. I'd do the same if I moved out to the Algarve or wherever – to / *Spain*.

NATALIE. *That's* your answer to all this? The *Algarve*?

LYN. / No, not the –

NATALIE. You're just *scared*. You're *terrified* of what you don't know. If you don't like it here then you're the one who should / get out.

QADIRA. YEAH!

LYN. Don't think I haven't *thought* about it. What *sensible* person hasn't? But I'm going *nowhere*. It's people like *me* who *stay* and *fight*. Thirty years I worked in that council chamber.

KASH. / We know. You've said about a *million* times.

LYN. It's *people* like *me* who keep the flag flying. Who won't be *silenced* by the naysayers and the do-gooders / and the PC brigade. It's people like *me* who keep Britain *British* and it's people like you who are *tearing* the *heart* out of it!

NATALIE *throws a drink over* LYN.

A moment.

NATALIE. Well that's silenced you, hasn't it? Actually. So.

LYN. …

NATALIE. Don't say another word. *Any of you.*

Beat.

She has the candle.

Now. I'm going to light this again and we're all going to stand here and keep our mouths shut and that is *that*. Okay?

Beat.

NATALIE *lights the candle again.*

Long pause.

KASH. This is my country.

LYN. …

KASH. It is.

LYN. …

NATALIE. Kash –

KASH. It is.

LYN. It isn't, Kash.

KASH.

NATALIE. …

LYN. I'm sorry but it simply *isn't*.

End.

TWO: TUESDAY, WEDNESDAY… FRIDAY

Tuesday

17. Bradford Interchange.

SHAFIQ *standing in a sea of rubbish with a sizeable length of timber.* KASH *trying to stop him going inside.*

SHAFIQ. They wanna bus their best fighters up here on coaches with Union Jacks in every window they can *bring* it, brother! This is *our* city. We're not gonna let them get *near* that camp. Police should never have let them leave Luton or London or wherever they came from in the first place.

KASH. They're not going to let them off the coaches. Leave it to the / police.

SHAFIQ. Yeah cos we can trust *them* after what happened yesterday.

KASH. It was supposed to be a *memorial* march!

SHAFIQ. They put *three* of our lads in hospital!

KASH. They shouldn't have *reacted* like that.

SHAFIQ. Whose side are you *on*? You saying she *fell* too?

KASH. You go in there like that and it'll look / like –

SHAFIQ. I don't *care* how it looks!

KASH. Shafiq. *Think!* They know about Nas, don't they? They know your brother's over there and he can't come back.

SHAFIQ. So *what*?

KASH. So who looks after your mum when you pile into the first person / you see?

SHAFIQ. Not gonna 'pile into' the *first* / person I –

KASH. Yeah?

   KASH *shoves him.*

When they do *that*? When they do this –

Shoves him harder and SHAFIQ *raises the wood.*

See? You won't even think about it. You'll just *react*. What happened after the riots? They went door to door. You've come up here *carrying* that – it's intent. Who looks after your mum then? *Think.* They'll turn the buses round and send them *back*.

SHAFIQ. Then why *haven't* they then?

KASH. It takes *time*.

SHAFIQ. Why *does* it?

KASH. I don't *know* why, Shafiq.

SHAFIQ. They're clearing the camp today. You reckon they'll just pack up and leave? Get home. Look to your women. Get your Qadira out that camp.

KASH. What?

SHAFIQ. Did you not know? *Behanchod.*

KASH. She hasn't been in that camp.

SHAFIQ. You had *no idea*, did you brother?

KASH. You're lying.

SHAFIQ. Both your women been in there! Least Natalie *did* something. Showed her *face* on a national *paper*.

KASH. As opposed to *what*?

SHAFIQ. All your *hiding* indoors, brother. All your *talking*, your *chatting*. Your *gora* / meetings.

KASH. Don't *talk* to me / like that.

SHAFIQ. If you're not gonna come in there with me and protect this place then *fuck off* out the way, cos it's not gonna be pretty.

18. HR.

MONICA *is very made-up, very middle-aged. She's clipped and secretarial.*

MONICA. There have been several complaints.

NATALIE. It was only *yesterday*.

MONICA. Still.

NATALIE. Complaints about what?

MONICA. Your suitability.

NATALIE. To what?

MONICA (*correcting*). *For* what?

NATALIE. *For* what then?

MONICA. Your role.

NATALIE. As a tutor?

MONICA. There have been questions.

NATALIE. About what?

MONICA. Your loyalties. The flag in the picture.

NATALIE. I didn't even see it!

MONICA. Nevertheless, it is *their* flag.

NATALIE. I've got nothing to *do* with them!

MONICA. That's not how it looked.

NATALIE. I don't.

MONICA. *I* know that.

NATALIE. Do you?

MONICA. Of course.

NATALIE. You don't believe me.

MONICA. …

NATALIE. So what, then?

MONICA. We have to reassign Jason and Stacee.

NATALIE. But Jason's *unrecognisable*. He's nearly back in *school*. It's taken *months* to get him to trust me, to get him back on / track.

MONICA. It's out of my hands.

NATALIE. I'm not so bothered about Stacee. I mean, not being – . But *Jason* – .

MONICA. We have to reassign Shamima too.

NATALIE. Shamima? I thought it was only parents who were – . *Shamima?*

MONICA. Her dad was very clear.

NATALIE. But I know him, I see him at the mosque.

MONICA. He wanted her assigning to someone else.

NATALIE. Because of the picture?

MONICA. He said he didn't want his daughter being radicalised.

NATALIE.

MONICA. ?

NATALIE. Two years I've *dragged* Shamima through her GCSEs to get her into a sixth form that'll take her, a sixth form that ran a mile when they saw the state of her school reports and I lose her after all that because I've been in some *picture*?

MONICA. What did you expect? Did it never occur to you that something like this / could happen?

NATALIE. / I didn't even know they'd taken it!

MONICA. I nearly got caught in it yesterday when that march for that woman was disrupted by those thugs – I had to go *right* round Lister Park. I daren't even go to *Greggs* because there's rival gangs of youths patrolling the streets. / I mean –

NATALIE. *No.* I didn't think about Islamophobic parents.

MONICA. I never said they were / *Islamophobic*.

NATALIE. About the *Ashrafs* not wanting me to *radicalise* their daughter.

MONICA. Well maybe you *should* have.

NATALIE. ?

MONICA. I'm sorry but – . I'm afraid we – . *I* – . Have to suspend you.

NATALIE. Suspend me?

MONICA. Until we've reviewed the situation.

NATALIE. What 'situation'?

MONICA. The young people we work with are very / vulnerable.

NATALIE. *I'm the one that works with them.*

MONICA. There's no need to be / like *that*.

NATALIE. Who are you to tell me what to do?

MONICA. / Excuse me?

NATALIE. The *state* of you! Like you're off to play tennis on the village green. I bet you live in a village with a green too, don't you?

MONICA. / What if I do?

NATALIE. Some big house in Heaton or Cottingley. Some *rich* husband.

MONICA. / What if I have?

NATALIE. I mean you must have changed your name, right? You weren't *born* Monica were you? I mean what are you originally, what – Indian? Is this a Muslim–Hindu / thing?

MONICA. You're being very offensive.

NATALIE. Am I? Then you know how it feels. And I quit by the way. You're nothing more than a glorified secretary, you. Sat on your fat arse eating Maltesers and Mr Sheening your magazines all day. What? Riled you have I? *Good.*

19. Fast Food.

A red-pleather banquette.

KASH. I told you! I warned you! What did I *say* to you?

NATALIE. They can't *treat* me like that.

KASH. Why didn't you *listen*?

IMTIAZ. I've tried to limit the damage / but –

NATALIE. What, the photocopier was broken?

KASH. Don't take it out on him.

IMTIAZ. The newspaper did agree to print a correction but – .

NATALIE (*hard*). What?

IMTIAZ. Nobody reads them / anyway.

NATALIE. They *lost* me my *job*.

IMTIAZ. I know and it's iniquitous.

NATALIE. Iniquitous?

KASH. Not the time for / big words mate.

NATALIE. I've been waiting *ages* for you.

KASH. Have you heard from Qadira?

NATALIE. No. Why?

   WAITRESS *arrives in an England shirt.*

WAITRESS. Lassis?

NATALIE. What? No. We didn't –

KASH. Why you wearing that?

WAITRESS. Manager's idea. He wanted us in full kit but I told him I weren't doing *that*. Says it's cheaper than boarding up the windows.

NATALIE. We didn't *order* any lassis.

WAITRESS. They're from that guy over there.

NATALIE. What guy?

WAITRESS. He bought you three meal deals.

NATALIE. That guy?

WAITRESS. Do you want them or what?

KASH. We'll be alright.

IMTIAZ. I'd like to have mine actually.

WAITRESS. Well make your *mind* up –

NATALIE. *Him?*

WAITRESS. They're making them *now*.

IMTIAZ. Could I have mine in a takeaway carton?

NATALIE. He's waving.

WAITRESS. He says you're the woman off of the paper.

KASH. Tell him thanks but / no thanks.

IMTIAZ. But I'd quite *like* mine.

WAITRESS. *Are* you her though?

NATALIE. Yeah. I am. Yeah. Why?

KASH. Don't –

NATALIE. / What?

WAITRESS (*shouts across*). YEAH. YOU WERE RIGHT. IT'S HER. Thanks a lot, yeah? You've lost me a *fiver*.

She turns on her heel and goes.

IMTIAZ. She will still bring the food though. Won't she?

NATALIE. Can we just go? He's staring at me. Everyone's *staring* at me.

KASH. They're not.

IMTIAZ. They are though / aren't they?

KASH. Imtiaz, can you just – ?

NATALIE. Let's go home.

IMTIAZ. He can't go home.

KASH. *What* did I just / say to you?

IMTIAZ. We can't though. We're already *late*.

KASH. They're not *staring* at you. / I promise you.

IMTIAZ. They wanted us for two and it's quarter past now.

KASH. Yes! I *know*.

IMTIAZ. I get nervous when we're late.

KASH. Well do your counting thing. Yellow things. Because
we're going to be late. Really late.

NATALIE. So you're coming home?

KASH. I *can't*. I'm sorry.

NATALIE. Then what?

KASH. Qadira's in the camp.

NATALIE. What's going on?

IMTIAZ. They might pull the conference.

KASH. Well what am I supposed to do about it if they *do*?

IMTIAZ. / I'm just saying.

NATALIE. / Kash –

KASH. I don't have to have the answer for every *single*
question people put to me do I? I mean for fuck's *sake*! I'm
doing everything I can to keep everything together!

WAITRESS *walks on. Stands with arms folded.
Unimpressed.*

IMTIAZ. People are looking again.

KASH. Yes mate. I know.

IMTIAZ. We have to *go*.

KASH. Yeah.

IMTIAZ. *Now.*

KASH. *Look –*

IMTIAZ. I'm just saying.

KASH. I know.

IMTIAZ. But we do!

KASH. Okay! Alright. Look. You go to the hotel and I'll see you there. Just – . No. Imtiaz. Just *go*. You get yourself home and I'll be back as soon as I can.

NATALIE. Where are you going? Kash?

He's gone.

20. The Fence.

They are separated by the fence.

KASH. Walk away from me now and you're not coming back home. I mean it. I know what's happened. I know what you're up to.

QADIRA *scoffs.*

QADIRA. You don't.

Beat.

KASH. I know that we haven't been – . Since Mum died, that / it's been –

QADIRA. Don't call her that.

KASH. …

QADIRA.

KASH. Look. When you're young, some things can seem –

QADIRA *gives a short, hard laugh.*

QADIRA. What? No. Go on.

Beat.

KASH. They can seem... important when they're not.

QADIRA.

KASH. ?

QADIRA. Did you get this out a parenting book?

KASH. ...

QADIRA. Did Imtiaz photocopy it for you?

KASH. I know you miss her. I miss her / too.

QADIRA. Don't. When you've brought *Natalie* into our house,
    into Mum's – .

KASH. Is *that* what this is about?

QADIRA. ...

Beat.

KASH. Look. I – .

QADIRA. ?

KASH. I know how you feel.

QADIRA. ...

KASH. I was the same when I was your age.

   QADIRA *scoffs.*

   I'd go up the ice rink with these lads.

QADIRA. The ice rink.

KASH. Four of us. We all had rings and knuckledusters and this
    one lad Waj had a knife. He had this walnut-handled knife.
    We'd stand about looking hard, wait for girls to come and
    talk to us.

QADIRA. Sounds shit.

KASH. One night Waj got jumped by these lads. He took his knife to one of them. Managed to get them off him. He was terrified the police'd get him so he gave me the knife to hide.

QADIRA. I couldn't give a fuck. / I don't need some *story*.

KASH. I just took it. The knife. Hid it in a shoebox under my bed. And the lad died. His parents were on telly talking about it. And I wanted to take that knife and bury it up on the moors but I *couldn't*. I had to keep it under my bed and try and sleep every night.

QADIRA (*sarcasm*). Oh well that's – . *Wow*. *That* changes *everything*.

KASH. Some things you take on you can't get rid of.

QADIRA. Is it hard?

KASH. …

QADIRA. Talking like this.

KASH. / It's nice.

QADIRA. Cos you *don't* talk to me, you just tell me off. So if this is *hard* it's probably because you're not shouting at me.

Beat.

KASH. I know… I was angry about your / exams but –

QADIRA. It's not just the *exams*, it's *everything*!

Beat.

KASH. I've still got Waj's knife. Still in that box.

QADIRA.

KASH. You can walk away. I promise you. Whatever you're doing, you can leave. I'll make it alright.

QADIRA.

KASH. They're clearing the camp. They'll be here any minute. Chuck us your bag over let's get out of here, eh?

QADIRA.

KASH. Come on. Chuck us your bag and climb over, yeah?

QADIRA. ...

KASH. What?

QADIRA. See you, *abba*.

She walks away.

KASH. No – . Qadira – don't. Qadira – please.

She's gone.

Qadira!

He punches the fence.

21. Shoe Rack.

Packed full. AMIR *struggles with the laces on his shoes.*

AMIR. They're clearing the camp.

NATALIE. Please –

AMIR. They're about to go in.

NATALIE. I've – . Do you have a solicitor?

AMIR. For what?

NATALIE. If you've been discriminated against. If you've been
a victim.

AMIR. Of what?

NATALIE. Islamophobia.

AMIR. You've barely been a Muslim a week.

NATALIE. It's not *funny*. I've *lost* my *job*. You're not even
listening.

AMIR. Let's talk on the way yeah?

NATALIE. Where've you been? I've been waiting hours.
Random people have started coming up to me saying stuff. I
thought I'd feel safe here. But I sat on the stairs in the hall
and brothers kept walking past and the *looks* I kept getting
from them. It's like – the temperature's changed. With the
camp. With the war on over there. Everyone's got something
to say about what I've done. Tell me what I can't do. Who I
am. *Nobody* has been happy for me. Not *one* / person.

AMIR. Natalie –

NATALIE. I got chased up here by skinheads!

AMIR. Stop.

NATALIE. And do you know what they were shouting? *Traitor*.

AMIR. *Stop*.

NATALIE. No –

AMIR. *Submit*.

NATALIE. I'm just – . It's all / a bit –

AMIR. / Stop questioning. Submit to His will.

NATALIE. Kash's daughter hates me. I walked out of my job.
The *one thing* that I've had. People *talk* to me funny. Like
I'm foreign. Like I'm famous. After the picture. Why does
anyone care about *me*? The *abuse* I've *had* in the street and –

AMIR *puts a hand on her shoulder.*

AMIR. *Allah* knows best.

NATALIE. I just – . I don't –

AMIR. We're all in His hands.

NATALIE. I know. I just – .

AMIR. He knows. He *knows*. Forget about solicitors. If
someone stares at you, smile back at them, yeah? Because
that says I'm here, I'm a person, I've got feelings like you
have. People are scared with what's happening in the name
of Islam over there. We have to remind those people that
we're *human*. We're not 'them', we're not 'it', we're not

'that'. We're here with them, alongside them. We're worried too. So smile. Be yourself.

NATALIE. But –

AMIR. Stop. Come me with me. To the camp. Now. We're all going down from here to do *salat* together. Brothers and sisters from mosques all over the city.

NATALIE. / But they're clearing it!

AMIR. We're going to get down on our knees in the square in front of the police horses and the riot squads and we're going to pray for *peace*.

NATALIE. There's –

AMIR. Natalie. Stop. Open your heart. *Allah* knows best. Put yourself in His hands. He's here. He's as close to you as the vein in your neck. Yeah?

Beat.

Good. Now. *Smile.*

22. Tent.

QADIRA. You going to *tell* me or *what* then?

SISTER. Where've you been?

QADIRA. Nowhere.

SISTER. You been crying?

QADIRA. Have I *fuck*.

SISTER. Whose tent is this anyway?

QADIRA. Does it *matter*?

SISTER.

QADIRA. You going to *tell* me or *what*?

SISTER *produces a laminated pass on a lanyard and a key card.*

SISTER. These will get you in.

QADIRA. In *where*?

SISTER.

QADIRA. Oh.

SISTER. ?

QADIRA. Right. So it's – ? Right.

SISTER.

QADIRA. What happens after?

SISTER. That's not for us to know.

QADIRA. But –

SISTER. We need to get out of here.

QADIRA. Yeah but –

SISTER. You having doubts?

QADIRA.

SISTER. Qadira –

QADIRA. We need to get the bag.

SISTER. You were supposed to keep it with you.

QADIRA. Yeah, well, I *didn't*.

SISTER. ?

QADIRA. It's at home.

SISTER. Then we'll have to get it.

QADIRA. But –

SISTER. What?

QADIRA. What if my dad's there?

SISTER. You should have thought of that before.

23. Hotel.

Tea trolley stacked with takeout detritus and coffee cups.
JULIAN *is transfixed by the scene unfolding in the square*
below.

JULIAN. Too late! History's already been made. That's the first
water cannon ever used on the UK mainland. And it's being
used on my watch, at *my* conference thanks to *your* city.
Cheers! Pull up a pew.

SAM. I'm sorry. There was no alternative.

JULIAN. If you listen *carefully* you might just make out the
sound of my career being pissed away in the late afternoon
sunshine along with two thousand gallons of pressurised
water.

SAM. You're sweating.

KASH. I ran.

JULIAN. You're late.

KASH. Did my adviser not come?

JULIAN. They drove that through / the night to get it here.

KASH. Did he not warn you I'd be late?

JULIAN. Look at it *cut* through those tents.

KASH. What did you need to see me about?

SAM/JULIAN. The speech.

KASH. So you read it?

JULIAN. She read it.

SAM. And it was *great*.

JULIAN. We have some queries.

KASH. Sorry – I can't stand here and watch that and talk like
nothing's happening.

JULIAN. Most of the women have gone. It's the Sports Direct
fraternity that's the problem now.

KASH. The *what*?

JULIAN. I'd stay if you still want your / *slot*.

SAM. We know it's a difficult time. Your wife's picture / in the paper –

KASH. Girlfriend.

SAM. The problems you've had with your daughter.

KASH. / What problems?

SAM. The marches she's been on, the trouble at school.

JULIAN. We had to vet you.

SAM. Standard procedure for anyone who gets to stand within twenty feet of the / Cabinet.

KASH. What marches? She's only ever been on one.

SAM. We have her here at twenty, in pictures. You didn't know?

KASH. *Twenty?*

JULIAN. I guess not.

KASH. Can you *not*?

JULIAN. What?

KASH. *Enjoy* watching that so much.

JULIAN. This was a wasted trip. Us coming up here. I said it would backfire. We've wasted your time.

KASH. What does *that* mean?

JULIAN. Your speech. 'It's complicated rebuilding trust.' How's that going? In light of this? The PM's address, the whole fucking conference line, is 'Together for a Better Britain'. Sky News has had nothing but this on for the last *hour*.

SAM. Let's not – . / Okay? In front of – .

JULIAN. Sam's only here because she's been over-promoted in order to champion diversity. To *connect*. This is a fucking PR *crater* that can only be *crawled* out / of.

SAM. *You're* the PR / crater.

KASH. Look. If I don't need to be here then I'm off. There's
people need me.

SAM. *We* need you.

JULIAN. I knew you'd say that. But – do we? I'm serious.
Spare a thought for the farmer's wife in Tetbury, the boys
and girls in Walton-on-the-Naze –

SAM. / *Here* we go.

JULIAN. In Tiverton and Goring, Aldeburgh and Harrogate –

SAM. / He does this.

JULIAN. Keswick and Carlisle! They're sat at home watching
what's going on down there – the pitched battles, this shanty
town full of black flags, these gangs attacking the police –
and they're scared that this will happen where *they* live. The
last thing they need is being told off by you.

KASH. I'm not 'telling anyone / off'.

JULIAN. Come on. You are. You do. That's the *speech* – a
wagging finger!

KASH. There are kids out there who are scared and vulnerable,
who need to hear that it's all *alright*. That they're *safe*. That
they *belong*. That they're not *abandoned* and *forgotten*!

JULIAN. That might be what *your* people need to hear.

KASH. *My* people? Look at you! They're *your* people too.

JULIAN. No. I've never gone for *that*. I've never played *that*
card.

SAM. Julian this isn't the / place.

KASH. It's not a *card*.

JULIAN. Yes. *Yes* it fucking *is*.

KASH. How / dare you!

JULIAN. You don't *know* / me.

KASH. Yes I do.

JULIAN. You don't / know the –

KASH. You're a coconut.

JULIAN.

KASH. You're a fucking classic edition, fully deluxe coconut wanker.

LYN *enters at pace, flushed with triumph.*

LYN. WELL I'VE GONE AND DONE IT NOW! I went *straight* to the cabinets at City Hall and I took the sterling silver Queen Anne-style coffee pot with matching cream boat, sugar bowl and salver and I *marched* the *lot* across the street – and in the pandemonium no one batted an eyelid – and I bowled *straight* into that manager's office with a packet of petits fours and a dozen madeleines and I told him – I said to his face – I said – 'in this city, Martin, *in this city*, only the very *best* will ever, *ever* do.' It. Is. *Carnage*. Out there, let me tell you, the *police* are *everywhere*. It's like the *ninth* circle of *hell*.

Beat.

Oh. I'm so sorry. Have I interrupted something?

24. Kitchen.

NATALIE*'s top covered in blood. Her forehead's cut. There's kitchen roll all over.*

KASH. Keep your head back – keep pressing / on it!

NATALIE. I'm *pressing* as hard as I / can!

KASH. You're soaked.

NATALIE. I'm *freezing*.

KASH. Keep pressing. / It needs a stitch.

NATALIE. *Aaah*.

KASH. What?

NATALIE. I went down on my elbow.

KASH. Why didn't you get out of there?

NATALIE. I *couldn't*.

KASH. *What* did you *expect*? Gathering like that?

NATALIE. We were *praying*. Hundreds of us. And they started *charging* / us.

KASH. Someone *threw* something.

NATALIE. No they didn't.

KASH. That's what they said on the / news.

NATALIE. *Of course* they did.

KASH. Have you got *any* idea how bad this makes me look?

NATALIE. What?

KASH. Did you not stop and think about / that?

NATALIE. Oh *I'm sorry*. Undone your hard work telling everyone 'it's all fine it's all brilliant we all get on we all love each other', eh? Cos it's *not* is it, *it's obviously fucking not*. It's a *war zone* out there! These old women trying to pick up their *stuff* as it's kicked across the square – their scarves, their jackets, their little bits of stuff that they'd brought from home. This one woman she was *scrabbling* after these little brass photo frames, little black-and-white pictures of her mum and dad – and she's *eighty* or something and there's this – what – twenty-year-old *kicking* her in the belly, kicking her like he'd kick a football and her skin's as thin as paper and you can *see* the bruising, all dark, see it *blooming* behind the brown skin of her belly. And I step in and try and help her and *bang* – I'm down in two seconds, my arms over my face, my knees pulled up and he's kicking my back, and now another one joins in, punching and spitting and shouting – Muslim this, white bitch that – and then they stop. They stop because they've realised the woman – this old woman – she's not breathing any more and they start panicking these young lads – they want to get an ambulance, *get someone* and then there's this voice this – one of them just says 'lads – she's going nowhere.' And there's a pause and then they laugh – *they laugh* – and then they leave her. And then I'm hit by this jet of cold water and I jump up to run and – she's just lying there, this old woman. Her headscarf's come off and her hair's all fanned out. And then the water – this *jet* of water – hits her and it moves her like a piece of rubbish, like something being swept up on a street. It just pushes at her, inches her across the ground. And I – . I've been pushing forward, been *clawing* blindly through this mass of arms and legs trying to look back at her and suddenly I'm free of the crowd I'm free of the bodies and suddenly I'm *cold*. I can see my breath in front of my face. People are running all around me, panicking, screaming and then there's this beep, this loud car horn and I realise I'm stood in the middle of the road. There's a man waving at me. He's got a car full of people. He's yelling at me to get in and I do and – . And I'm gone. And he dropped me off just now and – .

Beat.

Why weren't you *there*? You should have stayed with / me.

KASH. You shouldn't have been anywhere near there! I *told* you to come back here.

NATALIE. The *look* in your eyes. I know – I mean *I know* it pissed you off – that I didn't give you enough *warning* that I'd decided to revert. That you *told* me not to go to the camp and I did. That the photo got taken and ended up on the front page of the – . I mean – I *know* you hate being made to feel stupid, being set up, so I *know* how much you resent me for that, hate me a little bit for it even. No. You do. You've got this fear of being laughed at, being thought badly of. It's funny – I mean, I like it in a way but it can be – . You can be like *ice*. If I've not done what you wanted. And yet, despite

all that. You do know that I actually – . Love you. Don't
you? I mean I know we don't say it. But. I do.

Beat.

And. I don't know. If. You love me.

Pause.

KASH. Qadira's gone.

NATALIE. Did you hear what I just said?

KASH. She's gone.

NATALIE. Well that'd do us all a favour / wouldn't it?

KASH. What's *that* supposed to mean?

NATALIE. She's a fucking *nightmare*! She comes between us
all the time! And you're allowed to tell her off but no one
else / can say a *thing*!

KASH. Well she's gone / now!

NATALIE. '*Gone*'? She just wants *attention*. I'm *sick* of it.
Being judged by the little – . Do you have any *idea* how hard
it's been living here? How *hard* this week's been? Have you
stopped to *think* for a *minute*? Why aren't you *happy* for me?

KASH. I don't know what you *want*! I don't know what to say
to people when they say congratulations, when they say
masha'Allah, when are the *nikahs*? It's *embarrassing*. / I'm
embarrassed.

NATALIE. You've got to have control over *everything* haven't
you?

KASH. No – it was *fine* before, it was *great* before but / then –

NATALIE. *That's* what this is about.

KASH. Then suddenly – without being asked about how I feel
about it – everyone's like – 'well when's the marriage then?'
Even family back in Pakistan! Even *they* know / and
suddenly it's like – . I mean. You've got *no idea* what I
protected you / from –

NATALIE. 'Suddenly it's like' *what*? I'm not your fuck-buddy any more. / Your little –

KASH. Don't do – don't be like that, that's –

NATALIE. / What?

KASH. You're being – no – we're not doing this, you've had a shock, you're being –

She shoves him.

NATALIE. What – I'm being what?

KASH. Don't –

NATALIE. What – I'm being *what*?

She shoves him.

KASH. Nat – .

NATALIE. What? You going to *hit* me? I'm being *what*?

KASH. I'm not doing this.

She goes to shove him and he grabs her hands and stops her.

I'm *not*.

She struggles, he restrains her.

NATALIE. Get off.

She struggles.

You're *hurting* me.

KASH. Stop.

He restrains her.

Beat.

Stop!

Beat.

I'm not doing this. I'm *not*.

25. Kitchen.

NATALIE *holds two bin bags full of her clothes. A Mexican stand-off.*

NATALIE. What you doing?

QADIRA. What *you* doing?

NATALIE. It's the middle of the night.

QADIRA. Forgot something.

NATALIE. Your dad thinks you've left.

QADIRA. What if I have? What do *you* care?

NATALIE. Who's this?

QADIRA. She's helping me.

NATALIE. Helping you what?

QADIRA. What happened to your head?

NATALIE. What do you care?

QADIRA.

NATALIE. You got what you wanted.

She indicates the bags.

I'm moving out.

QADIRA. Better off without him.

NATALIE. Sorry who are you again?

QADIRA. Helen.

NATALIE. Right.

QADIRA. We should probably –

NATALIE. 'Helen'?

QADIRA. Yeah.

NATALIE. You staying at Helen's, are you?

QADIRA. Yeah. We need to / go.

NATALIE. *Helen?*

QADIRA. Yeah.

NATALIE. Does she not speak for herself?

SISTER. ...

NATALIE. What's in the bag?

QADIRA. Nothing.

NATALIE. Where are you going?

QADIRA. Nowhere.

NATALIE. Your dad's worried about you.

QADIRA. So what?

NATALIE. He said you're involved in / something.

QADIRA. He's a dick.

NATALIE. ?

QADIRA. I'm just making a *point*. Just teaching him a lesson.

NATALIE. ...

QADIRA. I'll be back in a couple of days.

NATALIE. Yeah / but –

QADIRA. You won't be here anyway, will you?

Beat.

NATALIE. Promise me you'll be safe.

QADIRA. What do you care?

NATALIE. Promise me.

QADIRA *scoffs*.

Qadira –

QADIRA. 'I'll be safe.'

NATALIE. And you.

QADIRA. ?

NATALIE. 'Helen.' Promise me.

SISTER. …

NATALIE. Promise me she'll be safe or I swear to god I'll –

SISTER. She'll be safe.

NATALIE. She'd fucking better be.

Wednesday

26. Secure Zone.

An anteroom leading on to the stage. LYN *dressed immaculately, on hands and knees, attacking a stain with a silver crumb sweeper. All three wear lanyards.*

SAM. They didn't let you through with *that*, did they?

LYN. It won't come out.

SAM. Security keep *missing* things.

JULIAN. He won't notice.

LYN. *I'll* notice.

SAM. They didn't let you through and not find / *that*?

LYN. It was *here*. On a table – over there.

SAM. They're a *liability*.

LYN. Is that better? I can't tell any more.

SAM. He's not coming through here now anyway.

LYN (*to* JULIAN). But you *said*.

JULIAN. It's not up to me any more.

LYN. Where is he now?

SAM. Coming from the Defence Panel. Minutes away.

LYN. Well why not bring him / through *here*?

SAM. We need him out front. People are still on the fence about sending troops in. We need him to make his *presence* felt.

JULIAN. There'll be drinks after. You'll be at the top table with him.

LYN. There isn't a top table.

SAM. Figure of speech. (*To* JULIAN.) And that's *not* in your gift.

LYN. What's going on?

SAM. Nothing.

JULIAN. There was a coup.

SAM (*warns*). Julian –

JULIAN. At breakfast.

LYN. I see.

JULIAN. A backstabbing.

SAM. *Behave*.

JULIAN. I'm not a dog.

SAM. I warned you. You overstepped the mark.

LYN. I thought there was an atmosphere.

SAM. I'm going out front to bring him up. We're a minute away. Then we can get Kash's speech out the way –

JULIAN. / Kash's *fucking* speech.

SAM. And we're very nearly there. *Julian*. Don't forget the extra chairs.

JULIAN. Your willing / servant.

SAM. Lyn, there's a local Party photo after –

LYN. Oh I *know*.

SAM. And I wondered if –

JULIAN. Don't.

SAM. What? Why?

JULIAN. Just –

SAM. I wondered if you'd mind taking a position at the *back*?

LYN. I rather thought I'd be down the front, with Joseph.

SAM. *Yes*. I thought the PM in the middle of Joseph and
Habibah would be a stronger image.

LYN.

SAM. We are keen to show how *diverse* we are.

LYN.

SAM. Is that a problem?

LYN. No. Of course not. I see.

SAM. Julian. Chairs. Lyn. Thanks. Good of you.

She goes.

LYN. 'Diverse.'

JULIAN. I'm sorry.

LYN. No. You're not.

*She gets down on hands and knees, renews her attack on the
stain.*

JULIAN. He's not coming through / here.

LYN. You can't leave a job half-finished. You'll learn that.
When you grow up.

27. Backstage.

Behind a curved, wide-screen, royal-blue cyclorama. We may distantly hear KASH *speak.*

Applause off.

QADIRA *enters with the rucksack.*

She undoes the bag and unrolls the thickly weaved Union Flag.

She produces a petrol can, douses the flag, liquid going everywhere.

She puts the can down.

Tries to light a match.

Her hands shake too much.

She gathers herself.

She strikes a match again – success.

She mutters something under her breath – 'Bismillah.'

She holds the lit match over the flag.

Applause spikes.

To black.

28. Hospital Waiting Room.

KASH *finishing praying amongst grey-plastic chairs and discarded rubbish. His shoes are off. His palms held in front of his face. The* SURGEON *is businesslike.*

SURGEON. There's a prayer room in the other wing.

KASH.

SURGEON. Sorry to interrupt. Her temperature's stabilising. She's sleeping. She's a lucky girl.

KASH. ?

SURGEON. I mean – that we were so close by. Better for her in the long run to be seen to so soon after the burns. It'll help when she's ready to take the skin grafts.

KASH. Are they *haram*?

SURGEON. …

KASH. The skin grafts? She'll want to know.

Beat.

SURGEON. That's not for me to say.

KASH. It's her face. Her neck. You know?

SURGEON. Yeah.

KASH. Her hair.

SURGEON. Some of the patches. Where the fabric had to be cut from the skin. The scarring might need excision. It would help the healing in the long run.

KASH. It's the smell.

Beat.

I can still smell it.

SURGEON. We've got a room. For parents. Why don't you get some rest?

KASH. I'm fine.

SURGEON. Even just an / hour.

KASH. I want to be as near as I can.

Beat.

SURGEON. Well. Mr Khawaja will be in to see her when she comes round. We'll know more then. And see that television in the corner? I'd suggest you leave it off, alright?

SURGEON *leaves.*

KASH *puts his shoes on.*

After a while, NATALIE *comes on.*

NATALIE. I brought some dinner.

KASH.

NATALIE. Hey.

KASH.

NATALIE. Some coffee. A sandwich. It's tuna. I wasn't really
thinking.

KASH. Where've you been?

NATALIE. How is she?

KASH. Why didn't you answer your phone?

NATALIE. How's she doing?

Beat.

KASH. I didn't see her. At first. She ran on behind me. I just
heard this – . Whooshing. People's faces – . Their mouths
open in shock. I didn't recognise her at first. It was the scarf
she was wearing. It was her mum's. It took me a minute to
realise. She'd stopped by this point. She was still. Her mouth
was moving but I couldn't hear what she was saying. Her
eyes were – . She knew something'd gone wrong. But she
couldn't figure out how it'd happened. She was like this
trapped animal. She couldn't understand where the flames
were coming from. I ran to her to – I don't know – smother
her or something but this security guy came out of nowhere.
Tackled me to the ground.

NATALIE. …

KASH. I hit him a couple of times but…

NATALIE. How is she now?

KASH. Sleeping. Morphine. Or something.

NATALIE. …

KASH. It's her face – .

NATALIE. ?

KASH. They used the wrong extinguisher. The security guards.
A powder one. For electrical fires. Clearly marked –
apparently. The powder – got in her skin. They had to wash
the chemicals out. Irrigate – they call it. They don't know
how much she can see.

NATALIE. …

KASH. She looks…

This is difficult.

Not – good.

NATALIE. Hey –

KASH. I'm fine.

NATALIE. You're not.

KASH. I just wish I could have stopped her. Just – *stopped* her.

NATALIE. Me too.

KASH. What?

NATALIE. …

KASH. But you weren't – . You couldn't – . 'Stopped her'?

NATALIE. …

KASH. ?

NATALIE. She… came back. To the house.

KASH.

NATALIE. Last night.

KASH. ?

NATALIE. For her bag. As I was leaving.

Beat.

KASH. She came back?

NATALIE. She was with someone.

KASH. You didn't stop her?

NATALIE. I was angry. After you'd – . / I was *upset*.

KASH. You *knew* what she was going to do?

NATALIE. Course I didn't know what she / was going to –

KASH. Who was she with?

NATALIE. I don't *know*. I didn't see her *face*.

KASH. Why didn't you / *stop her*?

NATALIE. I made her promise!

KASH. Why didn't / you –

NATALIE. I made her *swear* Qadira would be safe.

KASH. You fucking – .

NATALIE. …

KASH. You. Fucking. *Idiot*.

NATALIE.

KASH. You – . You could *have* – . You could have / *stopped* her!

NATALIE. I know!

KASH. She wouldn't be – . None of this / would have – .

NATALIE. I *know*. Kash. / I know. I'm *sorry*.

KASH. You fucking – . *Why* didn't you – ?

He kicks a chair. Takes his anger out as best he can.

A long moment.

My parents are coming.

Beat.

They've dropped everything. They'll be on the plane now.

Beat.

NATALIE. Kash, I –

KASH. *Don't*. Just – .

NATALIE. Should I go?

LYN *comes on with flowers, upbeat*.

LYN. *There* you are! I went to BRI and – . Oh. Sorry.

Beat.

The PM's office asked me to bring these for her.

She proffers the flowers. No one takes them.

Nice gesture, I thought.

Beat.

There's quite a scrum of them out there. Press and so on.

NATALIE. You should have rung ahead. There's a side door they don't know about.

LYN. How is she?

KASH. …

NATALIE. She's not good.

LYN. No. Who's her consultant? Apparently Khawaja's the man. Is it him?

KASH *nods*.

Oh good. Well. That's something at least. She'll be on antibiotics, I imagine? Infection's the real risk, isn't it? As the skin heals. Funguses. That sort of thing.

NATALIE. Mum –

LYN. *Sorry*. Yes. Of course. I'm babbling. Sorry.

Pause.

What did she think she was doing?

NATALIE. Don't –

LYN. Well, I mean really – *what*? All those years you worked. Your ambitions to – . And all of it's just – .

NATALIE. What did I just say?

LYN. Sorry. I'm sorry. It's just such a *shock* to see your faces all over the news.

KASH. What?

NATALIE. He doesn't / know.

LYN. Why haven't you told him? Didn't you see the PM's speech?

NATALIE. This isn't the time.

LYN. He mentioned her a lot – statesmanlike, sleeves rolled up. They're saying it's done him a favour. Stepping in. Facing the flames –

NATALIE. *Seriously?*

LYN. What?

KASH. Let her gloat.

LYN. Oh *Kash*. No. I'm not *gloating*. Hasn't he seen the news? Her picture's *everywhere*. Didn't you know?

KASH. She's a kid. She burnt a flag. So what?

LYN. She tried to *attack* the *Prime Minister*.

KASH. No. This was about *me*.

LYN. Well either way you need a solicitor.

KASH. I've spoken to one. He's said she'll get a fine, a suspended sentence. Community order.

LYN. They're saying they'll recall Parliament. Table a motion to support the Americans. The PM's making a statement in two hours. He wants *you* to be there with him. Both of you. Standing in solidarity. So. Stand with him. Let the world see what side you're both on.

KASH. What side am I on then?

LYN. Well – I mean – of course – *I* know.

KASH. Do you?

LYN. *Yes*.

KASH. You said this wasn't my country.

LYN. Kash. Come on. I'd had a few drinks. Let's not – .

Beat.

KASH. Young lads come to me. Nas came to me. About going over there. I tell them all the same thing. Don't go. Don't do it. It's a life sentence. I tell them we've got it good here. More mosques than you could need in a lifetime. You can speak *Urdu*, *Punjabi*, *Mirpuri*, *Kashmiri* in a hundred shops across the city and be understood. You can eat cheaply, live cheaply, buy houses cheaply. You were born here, I tell them, why would you go anywhere else? Stay. Work. Get married. Have kids. Put down your roots. But for what? To be *tolerated*? To tone yourself down so much you don't know who you are? There's a difference between blending in and disappearing. Some of these kids – the *lives* they've had – all they've been told is what they're *not*. They're *not* British. They're *not* Pakistani. They're *not* allowed in this nightclub, in this football ground, in this expensive restaurant because of the colour of their *skin*. So for them to stand up and say who they are, what they *believe* in, that's powerful stuff. That's a hard pull. And I couldn't stop Nas. And I couldn't – . I couldn't stop my own – . They don't listen to me any more. I'm *tired* of trying to hold both sides together. Tell you lot we're not a threat. Tell them that they've a place here. I don't believe it any more.

Beat.

So no. I won't stand next to him while he says he'll do what America tells him. It'll just be another war on a desert, on a people who'll get pounded into the ground for being poor and being Muslim. I won't do that to my daughter. I've let her down enough already. So – Lyn. Thanks for your offer. But if you would – could you just fuck off?

Beat.

LYN *places the flowers down. She's poised, dignified.*

LYN. They were expensive, these.

Beat.

I didn't need to come here. I wasn't looking forward to it. To you. I knew you'd be like this – no, I'm sorry but I did. I never met the PM in the end. They hauled me off. It was me after all who recommended you in the first place. So. They thought I might be *involved*. Joseph came down, his chain of office clanking. Sat with me through it. He's a solicitor and he made short work of that Samara. It was her plan that I come over. Joseph said it didn't hurt to show willing. I was grateful. So when she'd gone, I thought I'd save him the bother of asking and I gave him my resignation then and there.

Beat.

It's not just the three of you who've been touched by this. It's all of us.

Beat.

And as you asked so kindly – yes – I will eff off.

She leaves.

A moment.

Then the sound of missiles thudding into concrete buildings, gunfire.

Friday

Six weeks later.

29. Living room.

QADIRA *sat. There's a TV on.* NATALIE *holds a tub of ice cream with a spoon. She no longer wears hijab.* QADIRA *wears a compression mask – her hair is patchy and her face and neck are very scarred.*

NATALIE. The soldiers' eyes are all glowing green. It's infrared footage. It's our lot. They're inching down a road. It's dusty. They stop. There's the flash of a gun. They're being fired on. Everyone's ducking. Now we're in a helicopter, above, looking down on some sort of compound. And – it explodes in a cloud of dust. Back with the soldiers on the ground – all patting each other on the back. Smiling. And now we're back to the correspondent on a rooftop somewhere. It's windy. It's that woman. The annoying one. She's doing that thing with her hand. Some graphics of maps, the wider region. Showing the area that they controlled shrinking. And we're back to the studio.

QADIRA *prods her.*

What? Oh. More?

NATALIE *hands the tub to* QADIRA.

It's good isn't it, this stuff?

QADIRA. …

NATALIE. Never had a chance to do this before, did we?

QADIRA *prods her.*

What? Oh. Sorry. They're onto the football now. You don't like football all of a sudden do you?

QADIRA *shakes her head.*

How much can you see?

QADIRA *puts her palm out flat and waggles it – 'fifty-fifty'.*

There are some *Sex in the City* reruns on, you know?

QADIRA *gives her a look.*

I'm joking.

Actually do you mind if I –

Clicks off the TV.

QADIRA. ?

NATALIE. I'll put it on again in a minute.

QADIRA.

NATALIE. It's nice. This. I'm glad he asked me.

QADIRA. ...

NATALIE. Glad you didn't mind.

QADIRA.

NATALIE. I'm so sorry. For what happened.

QADIRA.

NATALIE. I just wish I could have –

QADIRA. ...

NATALIE. I should have done something.

Sound of door, offstage.

KASH (*off, brightly*). Hello?

NATALIE *springs up.*

NATALIE. Hi-i!

KASH *comes on. He wears a shalwar kameez.*

KASH. Hey.

NATALIE. Hey.

KASH. How's she been?

NATALIE. Yeah good, fine, yeah.

KASH. ...

NATALIE. …

KASH. …

NATALIE. You made good time.

KASH. Yeah. M62 in an hour, eh?

NATALIE. They get off alright?

KASH. Yeah. Fine. Straight through.

NATALIE. We've been watching TV. Not the news or anything,
    just – .

KASH. ?

NATALIE. I brought some Häagen-Dazs. Y'know.

KASH. Sounds good.

NATALIE. Yeah.

KASH. Look – thanks for –

NATALIE. No it's fine, if you need someone / again –

KASH. There's a carer been booked / so –

NATALIE. Oh. Right.

KASH. When I can't be / here.

NATALIE. Yeah. / Course.

KASH. So it's / fine really.

NATALIE. Right. Got it.

KASH. I'm not being – .

NATALIE.

KASH. You good though?

NATALIE. I should go. It's late.

KASH. Yeah, sorry.

NATALIE. It's fine.

KASH.

Her mobile goes off – alarm tone.

NATALIE. Sorry. Prayer reminder.

KASH. So you're still –

NATALIE. Yeah. I only wear a scarf for prayer. Made it easier. After the photo. After all that.

KASH. ?

NATALIE. And you look very smart.

KASH. Yeah. Well. You know.

NATALIE. You look good.

KASH. …

NATALIE. What?

KASH. …

QADIRA *gets up.*

NATALIE. Hey!

KASH. What you doing, *beti*?

NATALIE. Hey – don't – . Didn't the doctors say –

KASH. Yeah – she's right. Hey – . Hey!

KASH *puts one arm under her.*

NATALIE. What you doing? Eh? Breaking out?

QADIRA *takes* NATALIE's *hand.*

You want more ice cream? More telly?

QADIRA *shakes her head.*

No?

QADIRA. …

NATALIE. Then what?

QADIRA *indicates for them to listen.*

From a few streets away, we hear the sound of the athan.

They listen to it – sung beautifully, decoratively.

QADIRA *starts to pray.*

NATALIE *looks to* KASH *for a moment.*

Then starts to pray.

KASH *watches the two women for a beat.*

He smiles.

He begins to pray.

The three of them silently mouthing the words.

They finish at different times.

The three of them are side by side.

A moment.

End.

Other Titles in this Series

A Nick Hern Book

Multitudes first published in Great Britain in 2015 as a paperback original by Nick Hern Books Limited, The Glasshouse, 49a Goldhawk Road, London W12 8QP, in association with the Tricycle Theatre, London

John Hollingworth has asserted his right to be identified as the author of this work

Cover image: branding and design by aka (020 7836 4747/www.akauk.com)

Designed and typeset by Nick Hern Books, London
Printed in Great Britain by CPI Group (UK) Ltd

A CIP catalogue record for this book is available from the British Library

ISBN 978 1 84842 480 7

www.nickhernbooks.co.uk

 facebook.com/nickhernbooks

twitter.com/nickhernbooks